"Meryl & Rob's book offers a very clear, straight forward overview of starting and operating a savvy greeting card company and what it really takes to take the company to the next sales level..."
   —*Vanessa Harnik, VP of Sales & Marketing. Notes & Queries*

"What a wonderful tool for budding greeting card and gift companies. If we had access to this information when we were getting started, our lives would have been much easier. Everything you need to get started is right here."
   —*Cathy Henry, J-Dig Cards*

"An insightful, witty and comprehensive guide to the greeting card industry. This book contains everything you need to know to get started in the industry whether it be as a manufacturer or sales representative... Way to go Meryl and Rob!"
   —*Beth Safran, Principle, What's In Store*

pushing the
ENVELOPE

The small greeting card manufacturer's guide to working with sales reps

Rob Fortier and Meryl Hooker

CENTER AISLE
PRESS

New York · Washington, DC

To the people who design, manufacture, sell, love,
purchase and send greeting cards.

Contents

Foreword

We started MikWright Greeting Cards in 1992 while perusing old family photos over a cocktail. Since then, we have birthed, nursed, spanked and coddled our greeting card baby into a modern day success story. Today MikWright is sold in over 1900 retail outlets and has many licensed products in the gift industry. What started out as an organic goof has blossomed into a nationally recognized brand.

So now for the million dollar question: how did we do it?

MikWright's success can be attributed to creativity, good designs, good timing, good luck and good marketing. It grew to prominence with a lot of hard work. It also took some business sense and lots of help from our sales rep friends.

As a card manufacturer, your reps are your eyes and ears to the industry. While you are sweeping the warehouse and counting envelopes, your reps are watching trends, traipsing through pages of industry rags, and listening to informed buyers. They see and hear it all first hand.

Please know that good sales reps are very hard to find. People start working as reps for many reasons. Very few ever grew up wanting to be in sales. Most fall into it. Some are just mediocre, and some really rise to the top. They will amaze you with their tenacity and perseverance. And, they deliver the sales. When you find the good ones, hold on to them. You will find suggestions in this book to point you in the right direction, but the real work of finding and keeping those reps is yours alone.

In business, we are supposed to think that success is about the numbers. That is true. Numbers keep our doors open and our lights on. Numbers also pay for homes and cars and vacations. But numbers only go so far. In the end, it all comes down to the relationship. Your relationship with your reps is just like any other relationship in your life: you get out of it what you put into it. Working with reps can make you crazy, but if you stick with it, you can make it work. It can also pay off for your company—big time.

Pushing The Envelope is a no-nonsense, A – Z format that just may become the gold standard for industry upstarts and veterans alike. It is clearly written and easy to understand. Meryl and Rob write honestly and with a heartfelt passion for the industry. Whether you have been in business ten years or ten minutes, you'll gain knowledge and insight from these pages. You will enjoy, learn from, and sometimes cringe at their war stories. You will also laugh. We have to laugh in this business. It is just paper, after all!

Many manufacturers and sales reps would hesitate to offer the advice found in this book. Let's be honest: we are all competing for the same card slot and the same coveted buying dollar. But Meryl and Rob bring all of their experience right upfront, generously putting it on the table.

A life in greeting cards is a fabulous ride. Sometimes you wish it would never end. Sometimes you want to give up and move on to the next project. Day in and day out, we help people express what they want to (or wish they could) say. As a greeting card company, we use pictures and words to give people a reason to get up in the morning. The information between these two covers may well be the reason you got up this morning. It will guide you through the beginning. It will see you through to the end.

—Tim Mikkelsen and Phyllis Wright-Herman
   Charlotte, NC
   March 2010

Introduction

May 2005. My first trade show.

After several years of thinking, planning, creating, scrapping, re-creating, re-scrapping, and creating again, my greeting card line, Paper Words, was ready.

With my booth secured, I placed paid ads in industry magazines and the show's exhibitor guide. I sent out press releases announcing my new greeting card line to trade magazines and did a direct mail postcard to potential customers.

In preparation for the onslaught of buyers that would be flooding my booth, I purchased bags of office supplies—an economy pack of pens, three clipboards, four staplers, a six-pack of calculators, and a full box of order forms. I arranged for three friends to help me work the booth at the show. A fancy candy bowl, filled with enticing chocolates, was strategically placed to lure in all my new customers. I knew Paper Words was going to take the greeting card industry by storm and success would be mine!

When the doors to the show opened at 9 a.m. that first day, my heart was racing. This was it. This was what I had been working toward. It was show time! I stood at the edge of my booth with a big smile and waited. And smiled and waited. And then, I just waited.

After four days of mostly waiting, I went home with $500 in orders. Disappointed doesn't even begin to cover how I felt. My bubble had not just burst, it had violently exploded and left a giant mess. I felt like I had failed. What went wrong? What didn't I do? What did I miss? Was this all a big mistake?

I know now that I had fallen into a trap common for many new manufacturers: have a great product and the orders will come, right? WRONG! Having a great product is only the start of building a successful greeting card business. The product is important, but it's the people behind the product that make things happen.

So how do you, as a new or small greeting card manufacturer, stake a claim in one of the most exciting, dynamic, creative and just plain wacky industries out there? Welcome to a world of saucy old ladies, fart jokes, original creations, clip art, and wanna-be art. A world where your industry colleagues are old photos, doctored photos, and half naked photos. Let's not forget the handmade paper, full-edge bleeds, plan-o-grams, rack programs, extra postage requirements, baronial envelopes, and more glitter than should be legal in any U.S. state or territory.

When Meryl and I first started planning this book, it didn't take long to come up with the most frequently asked questions from new and prospective manufacturers. It also didn't take long to figure out the important pieces so many new card companies overlook in their efforts to start getting customers, orders, and sales reps. How do you get from concept to cash register? How do you stand out from the thousands of other manufacturers competing for a buyer's attention and dollars? Why should they buy your product? How do they know your product will sell?

The answers just might lie with the real driving force behind the industry— the sales rep. But who are these magical and often elusive creatures? How do you find them? Why do you need them and what can they do for you that you can't do on your own?

Sure, you could try to forge ahead yourself, but who has that kind of time? I don't know about you, but I got into this crazy business because I wanted to design cool stuff. Selling has never been one of my strengths—from selling candy bars for my school in third grade to going into stores and presenting my line now. I'm happy to leave it to the experts, and my line has certainly benefited from it.

That doesn't mean that I have taken a hands-off approach to selling Paper Words. Even if I'm not out there peddling products myself, I still need to know all the ins and outs of the industry, and so do you. You are the expert on your business, and the knowledge you possess about your company history, your artwork, and your line is invaluable. However, you can't teach (or expect) someone else to sell your line effectively if you have no idea how the selling process works and what your reps in the field are up against.

If you are a new manufacturer, no doubt you have tons of questions and few resources to consult. How do you find reps? What do they want and need? What do you pay them? What should you expect after you start working together? How can you make the relationship successful?

You are not alone in asking those questions, and that's why we wrote this book.

In the following chapters, Meryl and I will cover all the basics of setting up your line. You will gain insight from the experiences and perspectives of both manufacturer and sales rep. We will discuss ways to assess your product and your market position. You will receive guidance on finding and recruiting a sales force, as well as some idea of what to expect once you have one in place. We will share ideas for keeping your rep relationships fun and prosperous. Finally, we will address troubleshooting and offer suggestions about how and when to make rep changes.

You will get some war stories, too. They are all true. We have changed or omitted any incriminating details, but we're giving it to you straight—the good, the bad, the ugly and the just plain funny.

In any business, you are going to make a zillion mistakes. While there are some lessons you can only learn from experience, we hope that by giving you the nitty-gritty of working with reps, we can help you avoid some of the pitfalls. Starting, running, and growing a greeting card company is tricky work. Add the selling component and you've got one tough job, and maybe one you don't really want. That's when you turn to the sales professionals.

Through this book we want to help move sales from being one of the most frustrating parts of your business to being the best part of your business. Sales reps can be valuable assets, and if you do it right, they will assist you in building a business you can brag about all the way to the bank. The rustling of paper is sweet, but the sound of cha-ching is the real dessert.

Here's to your success!

—Rob Fortier
New York, NY
March 2010

PART
ONE

The Business of Cards 1.0

CHAPTER

1

Building Your House of Cards

So, you wanna work with reps.

This is a big decision, and often a pivotal move for a small card manufacturer. In order to work with sales reps, you have to be prepared. Successful and profitable sales relationships require a certain level of product preparation and development, market positioning and good old-fashioned hard work. You are about to take your company from "me" (and your partner, parents and anyone else who'll listen) to "we" and, like any business expansion, you need to be ready and plan for success. But is your company ready to take this next step?

The decision to work with sales reps is not something to rush into. By utilizing outside sales representation, you are making a deeper commitment to your products. You are also making a commitment to the livelihoods of the people you hire to represent you. Your future co-workers are going to have expectations and needs. Along with delivering great product, part of your job as the manufacturer is to equip your reps with all the necessary tools they will need to sell the hell out of your stuff. You should also prepare to have a really good time working with some of the most interesting, quirky, creative, and downright funny people you'll ever encounter.

What is your role as a manufacturer? Up to this point, you may not have given that much thought. In fact, you may not even be sure how to approach the question. On the surface, the answer might seem easy: To design and create greeting cards to be sold by sales reps. That answer is a great start, but there is much more to take into consideration. Generating the product is only one small part of the picture. Before bringing in the sales reps, you have to lay some groundwork.

Life as a card manufacturer is a multifaceted existence. It is very creative, rarely boring and usually fun. It can also be overwhelming, confusing and even a little frightening. Unless you are one of those rare and very lucky manufacturers who happen to make a fad item that takes off (à la Crocs), there are some key areas you will need to develop in your quest to take over the world. Creativity counts but bear in mind that this is, first and foremost, a business. While you do not need an MBA to participate, you do need to have a sense of the overall industry and what will be expected of you as a manufacturer.

Finding Your Place

In order to sell your line effectively, you will need to first determine your target market. The card industry is a vast universe of nooks, crannies, specialties and nuances. Just look around in any retail store. You will see lots of wonderful, creative products. You will also see a lot of knock-offs and copycats. Then, there are some things that just leave you scratching your head and wondering, "Who buys *that*?"

Every successful product has an appeal factor to a specific audience. Certain people will only purchase particular products and there is nothing you can do to change that. So as you start to identify your target market, ask yourself, "Who is the customer that will buy my greeting cards?" Just because you sell greeting cards and everybody in the world buys greeting cards does not mean that *your* cards are for *everybody*—no matter what you think. Here are some questions to consider as you determine your target audience:

- Who do my greeting cards appeal to?

- How old are my customers?

- What is my customers' income level?

- What do my customers do for a living?

- Where do my customers shop?

- What types of stores do they shop in?

- How much are they willing to spend?

- What types of cards do they usually buy (handmade? photographic? humorous?)

- What occasions do your customers buy cards for? (birthday? wedding? divorce?)

- How often do they purchase cards?

- Is purchasing cards an obligation, or do they truly enjoy sending cards?

Rob says: I have a close friend who only purchases cards at the grocery store, and only if they cost less than $2.50. I have another close friend who only buys cards at boutique stores and does not bat an eye at spending $6.00 for one card. Both of these consumers are definitely in a target group for certain card manufacturers!

Do a little informal market research, too. Type up a survey with five or six of these kinds of questions and email it to your friends and family. You may be surprised to find out some of their buying habits.

If you are brand new to wholesale greeting cards, we highly recommend attending a stationery and/or gift trade show before investing a lot of money in product inventory. Get familiar with the business. Learn about the other manufacturers out there and what they are doing. Having an idea of the larger industry, as well as your target market, will help you determine the kind of retail outlets where your products will be most successful.

Attending a show will also help develop your marketing strategies as you decide where, how, and if you will advertise. Your motivational weight loss cards will probably not be well received at the Down Home Cooking trade show featuring Paula Dean. Spending time, energy, and money to get in front of people who will not buy your products does nothing to help your business grow. By determining your target market, you can avoid spinning your wheels.

The great (and equally unfortunate) thing about the card industry is that anybody with a few ideas and a few bucks can design and produce some sort of product to sell. Despite all the legitimate hard work and imagination that go into these products, not all of them are sellable.

You may think you have a great product—and your mom may agree—and you may believe you are ready for the retail world to start ordering from you in buckets. But before you can realistically start raking in the cash, you need to ask yourself an important question, one that will be a central, guiding force in your business: Why should the world buy *my* product? You may be the first person to develop a card line for Tibetan monks, but still, *why* should someone buy it? If you are having trouble answering this question or do not even understand the question in the first place, now is an excellent time to step back and figure out your Unique Selling Position ("USP").

Your Unique Selling Position.

Your USP is your Unique Selling Position or your Unique Selling Proposition. It is what sets your product apart from the competition and gives people a reason to buy. It defines your mission, your purpose and your identity as a manufacturer. While it is not quite a magical love potion that makes customers and reps fall for you, it is pretty close.

As we were working on this book, we had a memorable conversation with a fairly new manufacturer about her USP. Her card line is very similar to a larger, well-known manufacturer. The cards were charming and funny, but the manufacturer had some trouble with the "USP" question. The answer consisted of, "Well, these cards are similar to those other cards, but no one has ever seen the ones made by my company." She certainly gets points for confidence!

An important part of product development (and sales, in general) is giving people a reason to buy from you, beyond just your charm and good looks. This manufacturer thought that everyone should like her cards simply because she made them. Well, with all due respect, who is she? And for that matter, who are you? Unless you are already famous, you are going to need a little more juice in your USP.

To help get you started in developing your own USP, here are some questions to consider:

- What problem does your product solve or what do you make easier for your customer?

- What are the benefits of your product?

- What are the features of your product?

- Who is your target audience (teens, moms, sports enthusiasts)?

- What does your product do that similar products do not, or, why is yours better?

Features are facts about a product. Benefits provide the customer with value and answers the "What's in it for me?" question. A greeting card example would be: "these greeting cards are printed on recycled paper" (feature). Purchasing greeting cards printed on recycled paper makes customers feel good because they are helping save trees and protect the environment (benefit).

You should be able to get your USP down to one or two sentences. It is similar to having a business mission statement. The difference is a USP is targeted toward the actual product as opposed to what actions you are going to engage in.

Here is an example of a great USP:

Old Tom Foolery is a letterpress card company. When you think of letterpress, what comes to mind? Something soft and flowery with antique scrolls or leaves? A formal wedding invitation? Or perhaps a thank-you note your super classy friend might send? Our friends at Old Tom Foolery have put a new twist on an old favorite. Their cards are all text-based (no illustrations) and are really funny.

So, what is their USP? Old Tom Foolery—uncrappy, unsappy letterpress greetings. Pow. What a hook! Four simple words and you know exactly what you are getting.

It is a natural follow-up to explain that these greeting cards are elegant but funny. They appeal to customers who like letterpress and are looking for something more contemporary or even a little edgy. They also appeal to the ravenous humor market. See where we are going with this? You want to run to your computer and look them up, don't you? A USP gives you something to say, and a strong USP gives your future reps something to say, too.

Another example is Paper Words, whose USP is "greetings that go beyond the rainbow." For more mainstream buyers interested in greeting cards specifically targeted at a gay consumer, Paper Words presents itself as both appropriate and accessible. An alternate way of phrasing the USP could have been "gay cards without rainbows and drag queens and jock straps," but a bite like that may be too much for some buyers. You want a USP that both describes your product and is understandable to your customer.

If you are feeling stuck on this, take a look around at other card companies or even at other products you may already be purchasing. Try to identify those companies' USPs and see how they are using it to develop their brand. Start with major, nationally distributed products since their USPs are easy to identify. Then, look at some smaller companies that you will not find in a big box store. How does your USP compare? Is it easy to identify? Is it easy to remember?

One way or another, you are going to need a USP. Otherwise, you are just another card/trinket/gadget competing for a buyer's attention. Your USP may evolve as your line develops. In fact, it may completely change at some point. The important thing is to have a clear sense of what your product is and your specific target audience.

Look Professional

It does not matter if you are a company of one or 100. Looking and sounding professional are non-negotiable aspects of appealing to sales reps. The good news is this does not necessarily equal spending lots of money. While there is some financial investment, much of what you need you can do yourself for free or at a very low cost. Here are some specific areas to target:

Presenting yourself. One of the most important elements to wholesale success is presenting your company and products in a clear and organized fashion.

Your company will need business cards and a website. Your business cards do not need to be super deluxe, but they should include your company name, your full name and complete contact information. Websites, of course, are a bit more comprehensive and we will discuss them in more detail shortly.

You will also want to have price sheets. A price sheet is a page that contains information about how your line is sold. Specifically, how much the cards cost, in what quantities they are sold, and minimum order requirements. Some manufacturers include this information on an order form, which is perfectly fine. Regardless of how you include the information, you will want to have it in writing and available for your retail customers and sales reps.

Presenting your products. As a small greeting card company, you will need a catalog. It needs to contain clear, high-resolution images of your products, brief descriptions (if appropriate) and style numbers, minimum order requirements, accepted methods of payment, and company contact information. Your catalog can also include pricing information.

If you are better at designing products than you are at sales materials, get someone to help you. Find a design student who is looking for a chance to expand their portfolio, or get a fellow entrepreneur to design your website in exchange for free products. Be creative and flexible. You might be surprised what you can work out.

One way or another, your card line will need to have a printed catalog. Many companies also have a PDF version available and we will discuss the pros and cons of both formats in Chapter 7. Ultimately, it is more important to have well-designed and organized materials than it is to have expensive ones. We have seen some great catalogs that were done on color laser printers and business cards that were printed at home.

 Don't print information that may change, such as pricing, directly inside the catalog. You can use a separate sheet that will fit neatly inside.

Digital printing can be a great, not to mention cost effective, alternative to traditional offset printing for both catalogs and product inventory. Much like printing at home, digital printing is a process where images are transferred from a computer file through a printer—but with commercial quality results.

In traditional offset printing, plates of the image need to be made out of metal, then transferred to rubber, and then to the paper. Because of the set up involved, offset printing is usually pretty expensive for quantities fewer than 1,000 pieces. This can mean all the difference in the world for smaller greeting card manufacturers.

Website. It is important to establish an online presence. If you do not currently own a domain name for your company, go buy one. There are several ways to buy a domain. We like 1and1.com but many Internet service providers will also let you register through them.

We all love bells and whistles on websites but you do not need them to get started. A simple website can be more than sufficient as long as it contains information about how to contact you and has clear, high resolution images of your products.

There are all kinds of free templates available for creating and maintaining a website. Most of them are very easy to use. Your Internet service provider may have website building programs available as part of your service too.

Social media. It is easy and free to set up a Facebook Fan Page and a Twitter account and we encourage you to have both. We'll go into more detail about social media in Chapter 12, but for now, know you have lots of options available.

Email. Set up a business-dedicated email account. Once you have a domain, it is easy to set up a professional email address. Ideally, your email address should be YourName@YourCompany.com. Make sure you include your first and last name in the personal information field.

If you do not have an email address set up through your website, we recommend using Google's Gmail.com. It is easy to use and it has one of the best spam filters out there. Make sure your email address is either your full name (firstname.lastname) or your company name at gmail.com.

Unless it is your company name, please do not use something like SixCatsToMarvelAt@hotmail.com or SweetnSexy@yahoo.com. We have seen many new manufacturers try to combine business and personal email. Doing this does little to add credibility to your business and flags you as an amateur. Besides, it is much too easy and inexpensive to set up a dedicated email address for your company rather than to try and combine both.

No matter what email application or web-based service you choose, make sure your email account is open to receiving all mail. Some programs allow users to set up a feature that requires all incoming mail to be verified by the sender before it will be delivered. Please do not do this. Make yourself easily accessible. Spam filters are pretty sophisticated these days and most of the junk automatically gets redirected. If you receive any junk email, just manually delete it.

Sound Professional

Telephone. Have a dedicated phone line for your business. Landline or cell, it does not matter, provided you adhere to a few guidelines. If you have kids, try not to use your home phone as your business line. The last thing you want is your three-year-old, no matter how cute, answering an important business call.

If you use a cell phone as your business phone, do not answer the phone if you cannot talk, especially not to say, "I can't talk right now; let me call you back." That is why you have voice mail. Never take a call while you are doing other things, like grocery shopping or standing in line at the bank.

Unless you have products for children, do not have your (or anyone else's) children record your outgoing voice mail message. Speak slowly and clearly. Leave your fax number on the outgoing message and have a message that fits your products and lends your business credibility.

We are often asked if a toll-free number is necessary. There was certainly a time when having an 800 number was a real status symbol and gave the appearance of being a big operation. There is a fee associated with having a toll-free number, and you may not generate enough incoming calls to warrant having one. Until you are cranking coast to coast at a pretty high-volume level, you can easily get by with a traditional direct-dial phone number.

> **Meryl says:** One manufacturer I know said his communication breakdown for 2009 was 87% email and fax and 13% phone calls. His office does not even have voice mail anymore. That is something to consider if you are starting your business on a budget, or even if you're not!

Fax. You will need a dedicated fax line or a virtual fax line like eFax (that delivers faxes through your email). Customers and reps send in orders at all hours, and you do not want to miss orders because you forgot to plug in the fax machine or you were on the phone. If you choose to have a physical machine, be sure to choose one with volume control. Your life will be much happier and you'll be better rested.

Your Money

Most of your customers will pay their invoices with checks or credit cards. You are going to need methods for accepting their money as well as safekeeping your newly earned millions.

Business checking account. Set up a business checking account in the business name and order business checks. You will need business checks to pay rep commissions and probably some of your bills. You can order business checks through your bank, but often times they are less expensive if you order online through a service like ChecksInTheMail.com. In order to set up a business checking account, your bank or credit union may require proof of business in the form of a business plan, a federal tax ID number or even incorporation documents. Be sure to check with your bank to see what the legal requirements are in your jurisdiction.

Merchant account. To accept credit cards, you will need to establish a merchant account. In order to open a merchant account, you will be required to have a business checking account (see above). There are fees associated with a merchant account but we highly recommend establishing one. Credit cards are the best way to collect payment upfront, especially from new customers or those without credit histories.

Thanks to technology, you do not even need a physical machine to process credit cards. Companies such as PayPal and Quicken offer what is called Virtual Terminals. The procedure is simple: log onto a website, type in the details of the transaction and process the payment via the web.

Keep in mind that all credit card processing comes with a fee, which can range from two to four percent. There are many commercial services available, and you can also talk to your bank or credit union about what is best for you.

Making a Profit

Depending on the products you sell and how they are manufactured, your profit margin will vary. As a wholesaler, do not assume that you will make twice what it costs to produce the item.

Many new companies figure if they sell a card for twice what the materials cost to produce, it won't be long before they will be rolling in dough. On paper, that looks great but there are a few things they forget to include in those initial calculations.

You must take in to account the cost of the raw materials you use. If you manufacture handmade cards, for example, be sure to include paper, printer ink, as well as any paints, glitter or gems. Then, there is the envelope. Then perhaps a cellophane sleeve the cards are packaged in. Do not forget about a packaging insert or sticker that tells the buyer what the inside message says (so the buyer does not have to open the cellophane). Suddenly the cost of producing the cards has jumped significantly. This does not include the cost of the time spent making the cards either, something many new business owners do not to take into account.

Here are some operating costs to consider when determining the profit margin of your products:

- Cost of raw goods that you need to produce your product

- Time/labor—whether it is your time or someone else's

- Product packaging

- Shipping materials

- Credit card processing fees

- Commission that you will pay to the sales rep

- Office supplies, rent, insurance, and professional fees (accountant, lawyer)

It is important to keep your pricing in line with similar products, too. Let's say you are making hand-painted, watercolor greeting cards and each one takes an hour to paint and costs $10.00 in materials to produce. If the average retail price of handmade greeting cards is $6.50, you are in trouble before you even start.

You could certainly try to wholesale your cards. But, in order to sell buyers on the line, you will really need to stress the features, benefits, and added value of your hand-painted cards over the less expensive watercolor cards. Perhaps your hand-painted cards look great in frames and can perform double duty as a card and a gift. Maybe you are a local artist to the stores you are soliciting. If your pricing is higher than your competitors, be prepared to explain whatever it is that makes your product extra special and viable at the higher price.

> I recently met a manufacturer who was trying to sell printed photographic cards at a price point of $6.00 each wholesale, with a suggested retail price of $12.00. The cards were beautiful but the price was too high. If your pricing is not in sync with similar products on the market, they simply won't sell.

Pricing for Profit

The standard method for calculating a retail price is to keystone. Keystoning is when the retail price is determined by doubling the wholesale cost. So when a card wholesales at $1.50, the suggested retail price would be $3.00. The standard markup for greeting cards is 100% of the wholesale cost but some stores will round up a little to help offset shipping fees and increase their profit margin. In this example, they might charge $3.25 or even $3.50 per card.

How do you, as the manufacturer, calculate your wholesale price to make a profit? Here is an easy-to-use formula for calculating your retail price and figuring out your profit margin:

(Retail Price—Cost to Produce) / Retail Price = Profit Margin

Your goal is to have a profit margin of at least 70%.

For example, say we have a card company that retails its cards for $3.00 and it costs $1.30 to produce:

($3.00 (retail price)—$1.30 (cost to produce)) / $3.00 (retail price) = 0.5666, which is 56.7%

That profit margin is a little thin. There are two solutions in this case: raise your price point or reduce your manufacturing cost. Our sample company decides to use less expensive paper and negotiates a better price from their printer, taking the cost per card down to $0.85 per card. If we run those numbers again:

$3.00 (retail price) - $0.85 (cost to produce) / $3.00 (retail price) = 0.7166, or 71.7%

Now we're getting somewhere.

Regardless of what your numbers look like, take a step back and be objective. Do you need to rethink how your line is manufactured? Even though you love the hand-applied glittery stars, do they render your production cost too high to actually make you a profit? Is it realistic to hand craft every card or can some elements be automated? There is a distinct line between a lucrative product line and an art collection. Both are completely worthwhile efforts, but having a realistic understanding about your income potential is critical, especially if you want your card business to be your full-time job.

Your Systems and Infrastructure

Having internal systems and an infrastructure is one of the most important aspects of setting up a wholesale greeting card business. Take the time to develop a system for every aspect of your business. Here is a handy list of basic operating questions:

- Where will you conduct/run/manage your business? Will you work out of your home or rent an office?
- Where will you have mail sent?
- How will your merchandise be stored for efficient order fulfillment?
- How will you respond to information requests?
- How will you track leads and prospective customers?
- How will you receive orders?
- Will you have a minimum order requirement?
- What happens to an order when it is received?
- How will you keep track of orders?
- Which credit cards will you accept?

- Will you accept electronic payments (electronic fund transfers or EFTs)?

- How will you manage orders with future ship dates?

- Will you accept returns or exchanges? If so, how will this be handled?

- How will you keep track of credits?

- At what point will you extend credit terms to a retailer?

- How will you check credit references for retailers wanting credit terms?

- How will you handle retailers who do not want to prepay their first order with a credit card?

- Will you offer any incentives (such as free freight) to customers who pay with a check at the time the order is placed?

- What shipping service will you use?

- How will you keep track of which territories have rep coverage and which are open?

- How will you track commission owed to reps?

- When will you pay commission?

- How will you track which cards are top sellers?

- How will you notify your reps of top sellers, new releases, discounts or specials you offer?

- How will you notify your customers of new releases, discounts or specials you offer?

- How will you notify your reps about any styles or products that are temporarily out of stock or have been discontinued?

- How will you handle shipping discrepancies?

- How will you handle product that is damaged during shipment?

- How will you handle past due invoices?

- How will you handle invoices that are never paid at all?

Many of the items listed above can be taken care of by using a small business accounting system like QuickBooks.

 Use a map of the US and sticky notes to keep track of where you have rep coverage. Or download a blank one from the Internet that you can color in.

Still with us?

These are just a few of the elements necessary to have your business run smoothly. Other aspects we have not discussed here include developing a business plan, and enlisting the professional help of an accountant, lawyer, insurance agent and a personal banker. Depending upon your situation, you may have financing decisions to consider as well.

A little advanced planning will save you lots of headaches and emergency decision-making later. Your systems do not need to be crazy-complicated but you absolutely do need something more than "I'll deal with that when it happens." Granted, there are some things you just cannot plan or prepare for, but those should be few and far between.

Develop systems that will work for you and where your business is right now. Some of these systems might change as your business grows and technology advances. You might also find that the initial systems you establish transcend external changes. For example, Meryl still uses the same simple file folder technique for tracking leads that she has used for 12 years.

It is easy (and tempting) to spend a lot of money when starting a business. Please do not. There will be plenty of opportunities in the future when you will need to spend money in order to keep your business going. Do you really need that $200 receipt scanner? We love office supplies too, but save money where you can as you get things started.

Laying a strong foundation for your business takes a lot of planning, thinking, strategizing and organization—and that is before you even get to create anything! If all of this seems totally overwhelming, you are not alone. It is a lot to consider and anyone who has started a business has been where you are right now, including both of us.

If you are feeling completely buried at this point, you may benefit from taking a mini business class at a local college. Many community-based education organizations also offer classes specifically geared towards new business owners. The Small Business Association (www.sba.org) has a wealth of information available online and at its offices across the United States. Check out the Service Corps of Retired Executives (www.SCORE.org) as well. It is a great resource for business owners, with free and low-cost mentoring programs and workshops in cities across the country.

You might be thinking, "This is all well and good, but how does any of it relate to working with reps?"

In short, it has everything to do with reps. Most sales reps are primarily interested in selling a line, not helping you get your business together. Without a solid foundation and a functional operation in place, sales reps will not keep your line very long, if they pick it up in the first place.

In addition to having your business structure locked in place, working with reps also requires card manufacturers to have a product line that is fully developed and, generally, compliant with industry standards and wholesale expectations. Getting your line "rep ready" may seem like a daunting, massive undertaking, but do not worry. We're going to lay it all out for you, step by step, in the next chapter.

CHAPTER

2

Getting Your Line "Rep Ready"

Now that you are starting to get a handle on how to set up your business and the basics of product development, it is time to look at some of the industry-specific details and vocabulary you are going to need in order to get your greeting card line "rep ready." These are the basic elements of a greeting card line that reps will expect you to have in place. Your customers will appreciate it, too.

Product Details

Style numbers. Each card you produce will need to be assigned a style number. A style number is an internal code you create that identifies a design in your inventory. You will need to set up a numbering system for your cards that can easily expand as your line grows. You want a system that makes sense and you want to keep it simple. We recommend printing the style numbers on the back of your cards. This will make reordering your products much easier for stores—and your future reps.

Imagine you are the owner of Furry Pet Greetings. All of your cards are targeted toward pet owners, and they all feature photographs of furry animals. You might start your style numbers with FP (for Furry Pet), and then add a three or four-digit code. Start with your first card and label it FP001, and then FP002, and keep that system going until you have assigned a style number to each card.

Some new manufacturers create elaborate numbering systems. Please resist that urge. Go ahead and accept the fact that as you add more cards to your line, the categories may not be in sequential order. That is okay.

Be mindful that you do not make the numbers too long. Sixteen-digit style numbers may make perfect sense to you, but they are cumbersome to the retailer and the rep. Plus, an order with 48 unique 16-digit long style numbers is bound to have some mistakes. The buyers and reps will also hate you if they have to write out those long numbers that make absolutely no sense to them.

The best style numbers are between three and five digits long. Look at the difference between these two style number examples. The first is a simple numbering system:

FP001   FP002   FP003   FP004

The second includes the style number, the month and the year the design was introduced into the line:

FP00162009   FP00262009   FP00362009   FP00462009

When Furry Pets adds new styles the following spring, the numbers will either look this:

FP001 FP002 FP003 FP004 FP005 FP006 FP007 FP008

or this:

FP001612009   FP002612009   FP003612009   FP004612009
FP005512010   FP006512010   FP007512010   FP008512010
FP009512010

See how the shorter numbers are easier to read? See how adding styles to the shorter numbers will create a more uniform system that will be easier to manage? Practically speaking, which numbers would you rather write forty-eight times?

Your style numbers should not include every bit of information about the design. If you need to track copyright or design dates, put it in a database, not on the back of your cards.

Let's say the following year, you decide to create a second line consisting of handmade cards with glitter and sequins. Then, it makes sense to consider starting a new numbering system so that all your pet cards start with FP, and all your handmade cards start with HM (for "handmade"), or something to that effect.

> When setting up style numbers, do not restart your numbering with each category. Let your numbers go sequentially. I have repped manufacturers who have Birthday 001, 002, etc., Sympathy 001, 002, etc, Thank you 001, 002, etc. This continues for 11 to 20 different categories. To properly write an order, the category must be listed with each style number. You can imagine the nightmare of deciphering an order from a customer who just lists the numbers and not the categories. Be a hero. Let your style numbers go sequentially and cross categories.

Pre-pricing cards. The issue of whether a manufacturer should pre-price cards is a matter of great debate among retailers. Some do not care; others are very opinionated on either side of the issue. We know manufacturers who print their prices on the backs of their cards and plenty who do not. You will need to decide which route you will go.

UPC barcodes. A U.P.C. barcode, or UPC, is found on the back of nearly every product on the market. UPC stands for Universal Product Code, and it is used for tracking inventory in retail stores. A UPC code is made up of 12 digits and has three elements: a company prefix, an item reference, and a check digit. The company prefix and item reference are the first eleven digits, with the check digit being the twelfth and final.

The company prefix starts off the UPC sequence and uniquely identifies one manufacturer from another. It is assigned when a company purchases the rights to use a UPC (usually by an organization called GS1, but we'll get to that in a minute). A manufacturer has no control over the company prefix they are assigned. The next few digits make up the item reference number. Unlike the company prefix, this sequence is assigned by the manufacturer and used to identify a specific product. The length of the company prefix and the product reference number can vary from one manufacturer to another, but combined, they will never be longer than eleven digits. These eleven digits are used to calculate the data check digit (the final digit in the sequence), and is there to ensure data accuracy. The check digit is calculated by the software used to generate the actual bar code.

UPCs can be printed directly on the product or onto stickers that are affixed to packaging. We have seen it both ways. Some larger manufacturers print their UPCs directly in their catalogs as well.

Do you need UPCs? The answer is simple: yes and no.

If you are just starting out as a wholesaler, you probably do not need UPCs. Most likely you are targeting small retailers who may or may not use a POS system. A POS, or Point of Sale, system is a computer used as a cash register in a retail store. It can ring up purchases, process credit cards, print receipts and, most importantly for you, track inventory. A POS system typically involves a bar code reader that scans the UPC at the time of purchase. A POS system can also tell a retailer how long an item has been in inventory and when it was last ordered. Some systems allow retailers to create their own bar codes (non-UPCs) as well, so they are not restricted to only buying UPC-enabled products.

If you do not have UPCs, you may have trouble breaking into some retailers, both large and small. When I was first starting out, I had several retailers tell me that if I had UPCs, they would start selling my line.

There are two ways to utilize a UPC code. One is to have a separate UPC for every style number in your line. The benefit of this is that your POS retail customers can easily track sales by style. They can see with the click of a button which styles sold out and which styles are still on the rack. The downside for you is the high cost associated with purchasing all those UPCs.

The second way is to have one UPC per price point. A price point is a fancy way of saying the retail price of an item. So, if your cards have price points of $2.50 and $3.95, you would have two UPCs, even if you had 500 styles at each price. The benefit here is that you can get these UPCs for a minimal investment. The downside is your POS retailers can only track how much of your product they have sold, not the specific styles they have sold. Their sales report will only reflect that they sold 255 units at $2.50.

There are several ways to obtain a UPC. The first, and most official, is to register with **www.GS1US.org**. You will need to apply, pay an application fee, and answer some questions about your sales and the number of products you manufacture. The fee usually starts at around $750 to get your own, unique company prefix. The UPCs are also not yours for life; you'll need to renew your GS1 membership each year in order to keep using those codes.

The second and more affordable option is to purchase one UPC for each price point that you sell. There are several websites, such as **www.SingleUPC.com**, which will gladly sell you one UPC. You can usually purchase a single UPC for around $25, depending on the company you use. These companies do not manufacture their own products but make a business of selling each one of their unique UPCs.

The drawback to purchasing one or two UPCs is that the company prefix contained in the code belongs to the company you purchase it from. It will not be officially registered to you.

A new manufacturer I know, who did not use UPCs, had several reps interested in her card line. However, each of the reps told her their retailers needed her products to have UPCs. Being new to the business and not wanting to shell out a ton of money, she opted to purchase a few UPCs, one for her individual cards and one for her boxed cards. She then attached the UPC stickers, which she had printed by singleupc.com, onto the back of her cards.

Some large national chains require manufacturers to have UPCs with their own manufacturer prefix. You probably do not need to worry about that right off the bat, but it is something to keep in mind as your line grows.

Shipping Orders

How you ship your orders and your sales materials is a matter of personal preference, sometimes based on which shipping company can offer you the best deal.

Ground shipping services. We believe UPS Ground and FedEx Ground are your best options for sending orders. It is free and easy to set up an online account. Depending upon your shipping volume, you may qualify for additional discounts.

With both of these vendors, you can create an online address book and track all of your packages in one place. With FedEx, you also get a discount for creating a shipping label online. When you have an account with either of these vendors, you can give out your account number to stores or reps to cover shipping charges for them. This could be handy if you ever need to have an order or samples returned to you.

Be warned: Do not ship your packages through a retail shipping outlet, such as Mailboxes, Etc. Retail shipping outlets add on extra fees, which increase the total shipping cost to your customer. It is okay to drop off packages if you have already created the shipping label, but do not use them as your shipping service. Buyers are always looking for ways to keep their costs down and their profit margins up. Consistently high shipping charges are a reason for a buyer to stop carrying a line.

One of my long-term customers has a very detailed shipping disclaimer on his purchase orders. The purchase order terms clearly state that he will not pay surcharges assessed by retail shipping services such as Mailboxes, Etc. He even goes so far as to weigh each package his store receives and then check his UPS rate chart against what the manufacturer is charging. An extreme step? Maybe, but in one year he recouped almost $25,000 in shipping fees. He hired an employee with the money he saved. Trust us—retailers are paying attention to these things.

United States Postal Service. This is sometimes the least expensive and least complicated option. Flat rate shipping boxes allow you to tell customers exactly how much their freight charge is going to be. Packages can also be sent with delivery and signature confirmation.

There are noteworthy disadvantages to shipping USPS. Most significantly, there is no way to precisely track packages should a customer call and want to know when an order will be delivered. Delivery time for packages sent through the post office can be erratic. Priority Mail usually takes two to three days, but it sometimes takes four or even six, depending upon the destination.

If the mail carrier is unable, for whatever reason, to deliver your order to a store, they may just leave your customer a note. The customer will then have to go to the post office personally to pick up the package. The post office will sometimes try to re-deliver packages, but not always.

> I once had a customer call me in a complete lather over a freight charge of $30 on a $200 order. When I called the manufacturer, he explained that the order was too big to fit into one flat rate shipping box ($14.50), so he put the order into two boxes with padding. The customer appreciated that the cards were not damaged by being crammed into one box, but the shipping fee was unacceptable, and they refused to pay the full amount of the shipping charges.

Credit Terms

As a wholesaler, you will be expected to have a certain level of fluency in the language of credit. Most of these things are pretty straightforward, and you may already be familiar with them. When you are getting started, however, it can be a little confusing. Let's break it down.

When a customer places an order, payment terms will need to specified. Payment terms typically specify the amount of time allowed to the buyer to pay the invoice in full. The following are the primary payment terms used by the greeting card industry.

Net 30. Payment from the customer is due to the manufacturer within 30 days of the invoice date. This is the most common way invoices are handled. This is most commonly referred to as "terms".

Terms are granted based on a credit check. Most established retailers have a credit sheet. A credit sheet is a one-page document that lists the billing, shipping, contact and bank information for a retailer. It also lists anywhere from three to 15 vendors with whom they already have established terms.

To check references, you just call the vendors listed on the form and ask about the account's payment history. If they pay on time with other vendors, there is a good chance they will with you. Your reps can also help. Ask them how a store has been with other lines. If the credit check turns up a spotty or downright miserable payment history, you can deny terms and require a credit card or ask for a prepayment check on the invoice.

Some customers may want to use a credit card to pay for a Net 30 invoice when it comes due. Some manufacturers will only accept a credit card when the order is shipped. Others will take a credit card as payment on a Net 30 invoice but assess a 3% processing fee to the customer. You will need to decide on your company policy.

For new accounts, it is customary to require the first order to be prepaid with a credit card or pro forma invoice. A credit sheet can be submitted with the opening order to apply for terms on future orders. Your rep may ask that terms be granted immediately for their larger and more established stores. Most manufacturers will grant terms if a rep asks unless there is a really good reason to do otherwise.

Pro forma invoice. On occasion, a store may not want to use a credit card to cover an invoice and does not have terms established with a manufacturer. In these cases, you will need to issue a pro forma invoice. A pro forma invoice looks the same as a Net 30 invoice. It shows the products ordered and includes a merchandise total and shipping costs. The invoice is sent to the customer who, in turn, sends a check to the manufacturer. Once the check is received (and sometimes not until it clears), the merchandise is shipped to the store.

C.O.D. Also known as cash on delivery, this is when an order is sent and the shipping company collects payment at the time the order is delivered to the customer. UPS will still deliver packages C.O.D, and they charge (as of this writing) an $8.00 per box handling fee.

Other terms. There are other types of special terms to be aware of too.

2% / Net 10: A customer deducts 2% from an invoice if it is paid within 10 days.

Net 45: This works just like Net 30 invoices but the due date is 45 days from the invoice date.

Net 60: Payment is due within 60 days of the invoice date.

December dating: If you have holiday cards as part of your line, offering December dating can be a real incentive for your customers. Sometimes referred to as "dating", the invoice is due December 1, regardless of when the merchandise ships. Financial outlays for fourth quarter are significant for retailers. Since most stores have their Christmas cards ship in August or even September, December dating gives them a wide window to build up some cash to pay the invoices.

Special and extended terms are a great way to reward your bigger accounts and can serve as incentives to help grow others. Be careful not to overextend yourself in the process. If an account routinely runs late on extended term invoices, you may need to adjust their terms. Just be sure to advise the rep and the account of any changes to their credit terms. We'll talk more about past due invoices and collections in Chapter 5.

Minimum Orders

For the most part, the industry standard minimum order for greeting cards is between $100 and $150. There are exceptions, of course.

One new manufacturer we know has a minimum order of $250. She has sixteen styles in the line, available only in full dozens at $18 per dozen. Essentially a store would have to buy her entire line (14 of the 16 available styles) just to meet the minimum. That is asking for quite a commitment from the retailer, especially for a new line.

Another manufacturer we talked to does not have a minimum order at all. If a store wants half a dozen of only one style, he'll ship it. He believes that by not having a minimum, he gives the stores the freedom to order only what they need, what they are comfortable with or what they can afford. He also reports that new stores, that tend to start off ordering small, almost always come back and place bigger orders.

With all that said, we recommend you stick with a $100 minimum order, especially if you are just starting out.

 If a store asks me what the minimum order is for a particular company, I always say, "$100, give or take". Even if the company does not have a minimum order, my time is worth at least $20 in commission.

Minimum Order Quantities. Boxed notecards typically wholesale in minimum quantities of three or six boxes per style, though we know of some manufacturers who do not have minimums on boxed cards.

It is customary that counter cards are sold wholesale in half dozens or full dozens. Counter cards are those not boxed and typically merchandised on a spinner or card rack. You may hear these called "loose" cards, but the proper term is "counter cards." If you offer boxed notecards as well as counter cards, it is appropriate to distinguish between the two by calling them "boxed notecards" and "individual notecards," respectively.

Making your counter cards available in non-standard quantities, like 8s, will mostly just land you orders written in 6s or 12s, regardless of what your terms of sale indicate. Be creative in your product, catalog and sales materials, not your business practices.

Exchanges and returns

Offering to exchange slow selling or shopworn cards is an excellent incentive for your retailers. Shopworn cards are those damaged and dirtied by normal shopper wear and tear. An exchange is not the same as a return. An exchange is a trade out of certain designs for others. A return is removing product from a store and issuing a refund or credit. With few exceptions, greeting cards are not returnable.

Exchanges should be applied against an order written at the time the exchange is requested. For example, if a store has 13 shopworn or slow selling cards and they order 10 dozen cards, the 13 pieces are deducted from the total of the order placed. Your reps will take the exchanged styles with them from the store, salvage what they can to use as samples and recycle the rest.

We do not recommend taking an exchange for more than two-dozen cards at any one time. We also recommend requiring exchanges be posted against a minimum order. You want to help the customer but you need to make some money off the order, too.

Returns and exchanges for holiday cards are sometimes an exception to everyday return and exchange policies. We will discuss those specifically in Chapter 10.

We know some manufacturers who offer exchanges and/or returns and some who do not. You will need to decide what your policy will be.

Officially, I do not offer exchanges. Unofficially, if one of my reps wants to swap out certain designs for others, I'm happy to do it. It makes the rep look good and it really is not that big a deal for me.

Some companies even offer a 60-day, 100% guarantee on opening orders. If the line does not work in the store, no problem! The customer can box up the merchandise and return it for a full refund. By your reducing the risk to new and prospective accounts, they may be willing to take a chance on you.

I rep a number of manufacturers who offer a 60-day guarantee, and I have made this offer countless times to reluctant accounts. I have landed the order every single time. In over a decade, I have only had three stores take advantage of the offer. Just something to consider.

Exclusives

Retailers love to be the only place in town that carries certain lines. The greeting card industry is not as cutthroat as other industries, but you will need to decide your policy on giving exclusives. An exclusive is when a retailer agrees to carry a line and, in exchange, a manufacturer agrees to not sell that line to other retailers in a given area. This is sometimes also called "protecting territory."

One of my manufacturers that gives exclusives sends every lead and every direct order from a new account to me for approval. I am responsible for determining if there is a conflict with an existing account. If a conflict exists, I notify the manufacturer and they send a form letter to the account explaining the situation.

Card manufacturers seem to be pretty split on this issue, and we know plenty on both sides. Either way you go, you will be in good company.

If you choose to grant exclusives, you will want to be sure to track exclusivity privileges in your customer database. This is important information for your reps, too.

Building a customer database

As you start to gain customers, you will need to keep track of them. We recommend setting up a customer database in your business accounting system, such as Quickbooks. There are many types of Customer Relationship Management (CRM) software programs available as well but Quickbooks should work just fine for your tracking and reporting purposes.

Your database should include the store name, buyer name, phone, fax, email, website, order history (which products they purchased), as well as the dates orders were placed. When taking on new sales reps, you will need to provide them with a customer list for their territory. Having a database set up will make that much easier. Collecting and keeping this information updated as you go will also make catalog mailings and email announcements much more manageable.

It is also extremely important to keep track of leads and prospects in your database. For example, if someone hands you a business card at a trade show, put it into your database. Make notes on your conversation. Did you give the person a catalog? Talk about specific products? Bond over your love of Broadway musicals? You'll want this information when you or your rep follow up after the show. You may not have a rep in that territory, but when you get one, the information may prove helpful. You never know who will turn into a customer or when you'll need to gush about your great seats at a performance of *Oklahoma!* to a fellow enthusiast.

Information gathering may seem obvious, but a good friend of ours observed his trade show neighbor throwing business cards into the trash. This neighbor admitted that she did not keep track of anyone who did not place an order at the show, and did not maintain a customer database. We think she is making a big, fat mistake! Leads and prospects are key ways your customer base, and your company, will grow.

Many trade shows offer a scanner for a fee that you can use to collect information about visitors to your booth. I just have a spiral notebook and staple visitors' business cards into it. That way, I have a place to take notes on our conversation and no business cards get lost.

Much of this may seem rudimentary, but you would be surprised how many new companies overlook these things. By making these decisions and getting policies in place early, you put yourself at a big advantage over the competition that is just making it up as they go. You also make your line a lot more appealing to prospective reps.

And what about those reps? When do they come into the picture? Well, much of that depends on what stage your business is at.

In our experience, most greeting card manufacturers are not prepared to hire outside sales reps for the first 12 to 18 months of being in business.

However, if you have been in business less than a year, have the majority of the previously mentioned elements in place and have more work than you can handle, it might be the right time for you to bring on reps. We say, go for it, but be advised: you may encounter some resistance and hesitation from sales reps.

The industry is littered with the carcasses of new, promising companies that went out of business without ever paying a dime in commission, or became completely overwhelmed, overextended, and unable to deliver products to stores in a timely fashion, if at all. Most experienced reps have lots of stories about getting burned by new manufacturers. They may be reluctant to gamble on a rookie company. You can promise with your life that you will not be one of those deadbeats, and that may prove to be true. We hope it does. Remember that taking on new manufacturers requires a certain level of risk on the part of sales reps. Do not take it personally if they ask you to call back in a year.

No matter how long you have been in business, if you are severely weak in any of the areas we have discussed, do not despair. Please do not feel like you can't do it or you are inadequate. We have all been new at some point—just step back and reassess. Don't give up! A little more mileage, seasoning and experience, and you'll be playing in the big leagues in no time.

Up to this point, we have talked almost exclusively about you, the manufacturer, and your business. As we explore working with sales reps in detail, we are going to start by learning a little bit about their business.

PART
TWO

The Business
of Reps

CHAPTER

3

Life as a Sales Rep

Chances are you have hosted a party at some point in your life. You probably spent a lot of time planning a menu, picking music, assembling a guest list, and thinking about a theme, decorations and ambiance. Shortly after you sent out the invitations, there was a moment of panic: what if nobody comes? Life as a manufacturer is much like hosting a party. You know you've got a great thing going on, but what if nobody buys it?

That is where the power of sales reps comes into play. They are your celebrity draw. They bring the "A list" to your party. You can have the biggest warehouse on the planet, stocked full of the greatest product, but nothing—and we mean nothing—happens until a sale is made.

So, what exactly is a sales rep, and what do they actually do?

According to Dictionary.com, a manufacturer's representative or sales representative or sales rep, as they are most commonly referred to, is "a person or organization designated by a company to solicit business on its behalf in a specified territory or foreign country." More simply put, a sales rep is someone that you, the manufacturer, hire to represent your business and sell your merchandise in a particular geographical area. As a manufacturer, you may think the hiring aspect is the only angle you need to be concerned about. But, understanding a life in sales will give you a huge advantage in maintaining long-term, and most importantly, profitable, relationships with your reps.

On the most basic level, sales reps are the connection between the manufacturer and the retail buyer. They are the face of your company and your presence out in the world. Sales reps take your products to places that you cannot (or do not want to) travel to yourself, and they introduce your products to people you may never meet otherwise. Reps are a valuable resource to stores because, in addition to new merchandise, they bring knowledge of the local retail and economic landscape, new moneymaking ideas, and merchandising suggestions. They have trust-based relationships with retailers, some spanning decades.

Additionally, sales reps are your eyes and ears in the retail world. They see what is selling and what is collecting dust on store shelves. They are your secret agents! They can also add credibility and legitimacy to your company, even if you are just starting out.

Like great athletes and entertainers, the best sales reps make it all look effortless. Day in and day out, they schlep samples, lug catalogs and juggle appointments. They get stood up and forgotten. They get yelled at and held responsible for things that have nothing to do with them. Many reps are expert tightrope walkers for competing stores and high maintenance buyers. Most should probably be awarded honorary degrees in crisis counseling, financial advising, handholding, and life coaching. They cover their travel expenses, postage, office supplies, and spend endless hours on the road. And, for the most part, they do not gripe about it. They work long days, drive long miles and spend long hours giving out free advice. The order taking, display building, inventory counting, and all-around cheerleading are what they sign up for, lovingly and without complaint. This is the glamorous life of a sales rep.

Sales reps wear many hats with retailers, most of which have little to do with actually writing orders. They are friends, counselors, and stock clerks. They are drinking buddies, gift-bearers, merchandisers, and movers and shakers. They can also be relationship managers, budgeters, jugglers, entertainers, moneymakers and sometimes, pains-in-the-butt.

They have reputations, agendas, and egos (even the nice ones). They have personal lives, social lives, and families. They have responsibilities and commitments beyond working for you. And they have feelings. In the crazy world of wholesale, it is easy to forget your sales reps are real people.

As a small business owner and manufacturer, it is not unheard of to become completely consumed with your product and the selling of that product.

However, even the best reps are not selling machines that spend every waking moment thinking about your line like you do. They need a little care and feeding if the relationship is going to last and be profitable. Now, that is not to say that you have to be all lovey-dovey with your reps or that you cannot have certain expectations of the relationship. This is business and no one is in it for volunteer points.

Like any co-worker, you certainly do not have to like your reps (though we encourage you to hire people you like), but you do need to respect the work of selling. At this point, you may be thinking, "Forget that; I can just pop up a website and work the phones myself. How hard can it be?" You just might be surprised.

If you have long-term goals that include growth and expansion as a manufacturer, at some point you will have to enlist the help of reps. Of course, you may have some success going at it alone; but how are you going to service the retailer who asks to see a rep with samples rather than a catalog? What do you say to the interested account who cannot visit your website because she does not have a computer? These are scenarios you will encounter in the wholesale world. Our suggestion is to be prepared.

Types of Reps

There are three types of reps in the greeting card industry: company reps, group reps and independent reps.

All reps work for some form of commission on the orders they write. A commission is a percentage of the wholesale price paid to the rep as compensation.

Company reps. These sales people work directly for a manufacturer and are usually paid a base salary plus commission. Company reps tend to be employed by major card companies like American Greetings and Hallmark.

Most of the reps you will seek out and hire will be rep groups and independent reps. Unlike company reps, they represent multiple manufacturers and work on straight commission. For them, this means one thing: no sales = no income. For you, it means you only need to pay a rep when orders are written.

Rep groups. These are also called Sales Agencies and tend to cover large geographical territories. Rep groups can consist of 2 to 20 or more reps. Every group has an owner or group principle, who acts as the coordinator for the rest of the group and may or may not be actively working as a rep themselves. They are also the person you will primarily deal with for larger negotiations. The group principle may help keep all the other reps, called sub-reps, up-to-date on product information or promotions. Rep groups may hold sales meetings to help keep their reps informed, focused and motivated. A group principle may also help make sure that all of their reps are performing to their full potential.

Each sub-rep has his or her own territory to manage and will make the majority of your sales in that territory. You will work directly with the sub-rep on issues pertaining to individual accounts and orders. Sometimes, a sub-rep will also rep lines independently outside the group. Some group principles are okay with this; some of them are not.

Commission checks are generally paid out to the group principle, who then pays the sub-reps, keeping a percentage for themselves. We have seen this retained percentage range from two to seven percent of the commission paid.

There are definite benefits to working with rep groups, not the least of which is the size of their territories. They usually cover multiple states, some of which might not have independent reps working in them. As a result, they also tend to have a large sales force, which can generate lots of orders in lots of places due to their coverage. Larger groups tend to work with more prominent manufacturers and have an extensive, active customer base, which can really boost your visibility.

Rep groups in Los Angeles, Seattle, Dallas, Atlanta, Chicago, Minneapolis, as well as other major metropolitan areas may have permanent showrooms as well. A showroom is like a trade show booth. It displays products from multiple manufacturers, and buyers come to the showroom to place orders.

As you can see, rep groups have a certain amount of heft behind them. We know of many manufacturers who have enjoyed tremendous success at the hands of rep groups, and there are some fantastic, even legendary, groups out there.

But there are disadvantages, too. Large groups tend to have big line packages. We have seen some groups with more than 40 lines. As a small or new manufacturer, you might get lost or get pushed to the bottom of the list behind a manufacturer for whom the rep can write a $2500 order. If a group has a showroom, there may be a showroom fee attached to signing up with them. In terms of territory and the roster of reps, going with a group tends to be an all or nothing proposition. There may be a couple of high producing reps in a group, and there may also be some you never hear from. When working with groups, you do not have the option of keeping some of the reps and replacing those who are not performing. As a manufacturer, you will also be responsible for supplying sales materials to every rep in a group. In some cases, this might require you to provide upwards of twenty sets of sales materials.

Independent reps. These reps are just what they sound like. They are individuals who generally work by themselves and are self-employed. Unlike group sub-reps, independent reps pick the lines they want and do not share the commission. What they lack in size, independents often make up for in performance. They are their own life preserver—it is entirely up to them whether they sink or swim. It can be very rewarding and profitable for those who are motivated, but it can also be a little lonely. We know of great success stories from manufacturers who have used independent reps, and there are independent reps out there who have been selling for over 25 years.

There are disadvantages to working with independents, too. Since they are solo shows, independent reps tend to have smaller territories and smaller line packages. They may not cover an area as large as a group would, leaving geographical gaps in your sales coverage. An independent rep might only cover a specific city, such as Chicago, and not the rest of the state of Illinois. Or they might cover a partial state, such as western Pennsylvania, or even a particular telephone area code. Some do have larger territories that include entire states or even regions, though this trend seems to be waning. Independents may only focus on a particular niche market (such as spas or high-end boutiques) and, therefore, may not give you as thorough coverage in an area as you'd like.

Most manufacturers have a mixture of independent reps and rep groups working for them. As you can see, there are pros and cons to both.

A Day in the Life of a Sales Rep

You might be wondering what sales reps actually do. They make a few phone calls, drive to a few appointments, write a couple of orders and go home. So what? Why pay them a piece of your profit? The key to understanding reps is to understand that time spent in front of customers is only a small part of the job. Most of the work happens before the appointment ever takes place and after the appointment finishes.

Here are a few key aspects to working as a rep:

Research. Before meeting with new accounts, many reps will do some research to learn as much as possible about the store. They will find out what manufacturers the store carries, who their competition is, and determine what lines they rep that may be a good fit for that store. Some reps will even drop by for incognito in-person visits.

Phone calls. Next to customer appointments, telephone calls are the top priority on any rep task list. A rep's call list ranges from contacting potential new accounts to checking in with existing customers. There are always problems to solve and all kinds of follow-up calls to place. Depending upon the size of the account and the territory, reps usually contact stores every 4 to 16 weeks.

Other communication. We all know how time-consuming email and the web can be. Reps have to budget time for electronic communication, too. Buyers (and some manufacturers) expect an immediate response to emails and phone messages. Some reps maintain blogs. Others make use of Facebook, Twitter or LinkedIn to share information with their customers, colleagues and manufacturers. Some reps also send birthday cards to their customers and hand written thank-you notes to new accounts, too.

Information management. A big key to sales success is being organized, so reps need to keep track of all of their customers, leads and prospects. Many keep extensive notes on an account's order history, when they last spoke, and when their last appointment was. Some reps even keep records on buyers' likes and dislikes as well as other personal information. Like you, most reps have some kind of a customer database, and they are constantly doing updates so that they have accurate records. We discussed building and maintaining a customer database in Chapter 2, so flip back a few pages if you need a refresher.

Product information management. Buyers and manufacturers expect reps to have an accurate, working knowledge of the products they sell. With 20 or more lines, that is a lot of information to manage. Reps are expected to review materials from manufacturers, and make sure they are up-to-date on new products and promotions. Most reps have some sort of line management system in place, whether it is a binder or a master catalog file. It must be maintained along with their multiple sample kits. You can always spot a sales rep's car on the interstate; the back is stacked high with plastic totes!

Travel. Since the biggest and best sales tend to happen face to face, most greeting card reps have territories they can cover by car. Travel time between appointments can take a big chunk of time out of a rep's day. Every rep tries to structure an "appointment day", with multiple appointments along a travel route that saves time and gas. Depending upon the size of the territory, overnight trips may be necessary, too. Planning and coordinating efficient out-of-town travel can be a lengthy process.

Sending out catalogs. Some reps want manufacturers to send out catalog requests. Others prefer to do it themselves so they can be the first point of contact with new accounts. Sometimes a rep is contacted directly by a store asking for a catalog. Preparing these mailings and getting to the post office can be very time-consuming.

Preparation/homework. For any appointment, preparation is critical. On average, a rep has a buyer's attention for about 90 minutes, so efficient use of that time is important. Since reps generally carry multiple lines, they do not usually show every line at each appointment. Not all manufacturers a rep carries are appropriate for every sales call, and good reps plan in advance which lines they are going to show and how best to present them.

For existing accounts, reps will review past orders, notes from previous appointments, backorders, and the status of any credits or returns. They'll want to make sure the customer file is organized and that they have an action plan. Top performing reps will also take the time to come up with new ideas or suggestions for their accounts.

Sales appointments. For reps, the actual appointment is show time. This is where reps really shine and, for most, it is the best part of the job. There is a certain amount of socializing that goes with an appointment, but it is mutually understood that the whole purpose for getting together is to write orders.

Buyers are busy people and each buyer works differently. Some like to look through all of the samples of each line, and others just want the reps to write the orders. Some buyers will pull an inventory report from their POS system, ask the rep to check it against what is on the floor, and then write the order using that information. Either way, appointments require time and effort for the rep. They may only be able to see two to four accounts in a day, so there is little room for unproductive appointments. Because they have done their homework, the most effective reps know how to make the most of a buyer's limited time and, in some cases, attention span.

Inventory. Many sales reps will help a store by doing an inventory of their lines. Taking inventory is the process of compiling a list of products or merchandise on hand. This helps the rep make better recommendations for reorders and helps the store keep their product mix fresh. Some stores rely heavily on reps to do inventory of their stock in order to process exchanges and credits for shopworn cards as well.

Bookkeeping and paperwork. Repping is not all just fun and games. It is a business, too. Just like you, sales reps do not want to go to jail for shady accounting or tax evasion. They need to keep receipts and track expenses (gas, hotel, food, customer gifts) incurred while schlepping your samples, not to mention keep on top of their filing.

Tracking commissions. Even though they love getting paid, tracking and posting commissions can be time-consuming as well. It entails keeping up with what commissions they are owed and who has (or has not) paid them. They also may need to make follow-up calls to manufacturers who are late sending checks.

Processing orders. Along with taking orders during appointments, reps also receive orders via phone, email and fax. Those orders need to be written up and reviewed for errors, out of stocks, and discontinued items. They need to be checked for accuracy and completeness before they are sent to the manufacturer. They also usually need to be transferred into a more legible format.

Now, imagine doing all this for 20 or more manufacturers just like you. Overlay a customer list of 150, or more, stores, plus leads and prospects. Tired yet? This is just some of work that goes on behind the scenes of selling. Reps have a lot of work to do and a lot of information to manage.

At this point, you might be thinking, "So what? That's what they signed up for, right?" In short, yes. Most reps are very aware of the amount of work it takes to be successful. But they are also clear on the fact that they cannot do it alone; manufacturer support is a necessary ingredient to that success. Do not forget that rep groups and independent reps make choices about which companies they will represent. Difficult, inconsistent, uncommunicative, or disorganized manufacturers put themselves at a tremendous disadvantage. Notice there is no mention about the size of the manufacturer. Size has nothing to do with being nice or being easy to work with.

It is important to make your products easy to sell and provide great information and support to your reps. The more obstacles you can remove, the easier it will be for your rep to sell your line to the right stores. Be sure to provide your sales force with a list of your top sellers so they can make the right recommendations at their appointments. You may even consider providing two-part order forms: one copy that can easily be filled out and faxed to you, the second to leave with the customer.

Make yourself available if your reps have questions. If you have a day job, let your reps know. There is no shame in that. Just be sure to check your voicemail and email often and respond as quickly as possible. If it is okay for you to take calls at your day job, make sure your reps have your cell phone number, too.

Sharing is Caring

Like any relationship, working with reps takes time, patience, support, communication and commitment. Unlike most romantic relationships, however, you will be required to share the object of your affection.

Unless you are paying a base salary and commission, your reps will be representing other manufacturers who have the same hopes, dreams and expectations as you. Some of these manufacturers will be bigger and have a greater market presence. Your rep will probably be writing more orders for those lines than for yours.

It can be easy to feel like you are small potatoes compared to those lines, but do not let yourself fall into that self-defeating way of thinking. Just because you are not writing $3000 commission checks (yet!) does not mean your line is not as good. It simply means you are new, and it can take some finessing to get new lines placed, especially when budgets are tight and the economy is uncertain.

There is a good chance your rep is using the bigger lines to pay the rent, which makes carrying smaller lines like yours possible. It does not matter how good you are—a rep cannot live on an $80 per month commission check. So be patient and keep some perspective.

Remember, most reps are smart. They have a lines package that, at least partially, works together. Major lines often serve as a gateway for smaller lines. A buyer is often more receptive to new products when they come from a rep they already work with and trust.

Even if you have done direct mailings to stores, having your cards put in a buyer's hand by a sales rep gives it a whole new presentation. Buyers and good reps have relationships built on trust, longevity, and a mutual understanding of the store's customers. Having a rep behind the product gives it a much better chance of getting placed in the right stores. Plus, your rep may be able to get you into stores you may not have even thought of or known about. We have yet to meet a manufacturer who is not surprised by some of the places reps have placed their products.

I've repped a fantastic line of adult greeting cards for many years. The obvious retail outlets for this line were gay stores, adult stores and edgy, urban boutiques. On one of my sales trips to rural Virginia, I met with a little card store known for its beautiful, sophisticated and rather high-end cards and gifts. The owner wanted to see the "dirty cards" because she kept a box of them underneath the counter. It was generally understood in town that if you wanted adult cards, you went to her store and asked to see "the box". She sold dozens and dozens of cards that never even saw the sales floor.

It may seem intimidating or even threatening at first to have your treasured rep lavishing attention on other lines. As a new or small manufacturer, this does actually work in your favor. Do not be jealous or possessive. There is plenty of love to go around.

Competing Lines

If you are like most businesses, you want your competition to die. Not just go away, but actually be completely destroyed and never return. Well, get ready. Now we are going to tell you that, in addition to carrying larger, more established lines, your rep could also carry your direct competitors, or at least lines that are similar to yours. You can certainly ask a rep to not carry those stinkin' rats since they are a competing line, but do not be surprised if the rep will not agree to this restriction.

There are two primary ways reps think about this:

1. Repping directly competing lines helps monitor which stores carry which lines and avoids saturating a market.

2. Repping directly competing lines opens up the market twice as large for both manufacturers. The store that has only ordered the competition is now a prospect for you. Plus, there are some stores who may not even be aware of your line, having only ordered the competition...until now.

There is no right or wrong answer to this situation. What we do know is that ultimately, the market will determine which line is the most sellable. The products that resonate with buyers and consumers will rise to the top, regardless of what you, or the competition, say or do.

The Good and the Bad of Working with Reps

So all this rep perspective is fine, but what does it really mean for you, the manufacturer? What are the real, down and dirty advantages—and disadvantages—of working with reps? While this is not a 100% comprehensive list, it does cover the most important things to consider in terms of rep relationships.

The Good Stuff

- Reps can offer feedback on products from customers that you might not hear otherwise.

- If your line needs help, a rep will let you know.

- Reps have an established list of customers to whom they can show your products.

- Reps travel to and sell in places you may never be able to access.

- Reps make suggestions on how your product fits in with a store's existing inventory.

- Reps can make suggestions on how to display (and therefore sell more) merchandise in a particular store.

- Reps can demonstrate how a product works or point out the benefits and features of a product.

- Reps can answer questions on the spot for customers.

- Reps can see how buyers react to products and get instant feedback, which they can pass on to you.

- Reps can help keep buyers on track for seasonal merchandise.

- By anticipating a buyer's objections, a rep can have answers and solutions ready.

- Some buyers need to see products multiple times before they are ready to buy. Reps can make that happen.

- Putting reps in charge of the selling gives you time to focus on other things, such as creating new artwork or developing new product lines.

- Reps are fun people to know. They are creative and often innovative and they always have stories to tell about life on the road.

- Reps have extensive networks and can refer you to other reps.

- Reps will help your business grow faster than you ever could by yourself.

The Bad Stuff

- Reps have their own agenda: make money. Period. And not necessarily with your products.

- Reps may carry ten to 30 other lines, so your line is not always the most important (see the own agenda item above).

- Reps follow the path of least resistance. They like to sell what is easiest, which again, may not be your product line

- Reps do not like to hear the word "no." If they hear it from too many buyers about your line, they may stop trying to sell it.

- Reps will never sell as much as you want them to.

- Even the most organized reps do not remember all the details about your products. Rob has had reps call from an appointment to ask about prices—Meryl among them.

- Reps can be difficult and nonresponsive to your calls and emails.

- There may be long periods where you do not see any orders from a rep.

- You have to pay your reps a portion of your sales.

- It takes work to keep your reps motivated and interested, even if you are their best selling line.

We feel that the good far outweighs the bad when it comes to working with reps. We mention the bad here because we want you to be aware that working with reps can be difficult and, also, so you will know you are not the first, or only, person these things happen to. In addition to moments of sheer joy and feelings of victory, there will be times when you will get frustrated and you will have to make difficult decisions about representation. You will get your feelings hurt when a rep drops your line and you will hurt a rep's feelings when you drop them. You will spend money to equip them and not know if your line is even being shown. You might have to kiss a lot of frogs before you find true love with the right reps, or feel like giving up and just doing it on your own.

And then, one day, it happens. The fax machine starts whirling and the checks start coming. The next thing you know, you have new accounts, reorders, and your company is growing. Sounds great, right? But, how do you reach this point? As you might have guessed, working with sales reps can play a significant part in expanding your company. In the next chapter, we will discuss avenues for finding sales reps as well as ways to determine if they are right for your line.

CHAPTER 4

Territory, Customers and Orders

By now, you should be feeling pretty good about yourself. You are getting a handle on your business, and this whole rep thing is starting to make sense. Up to this point, we have discussed the independent lives of manufacturers and sales reps. Now we are going to put it all together and examine the working relationship between the two. There is some industry lingo you will need to learn in order to effectively communicate with reps. You want to be able to walk and talk like a pro, right? This information will be particularly important as you seek out and start talking to potential reps.

Territory

Every rep has a territory. A territory is the geographical area in which a rep sells product. It is the lifeblood of a career in sales. Lines come and go, but the territory is where it all happens. As we mentioned before, some reps have a relatively small territory, such as a city, while others might sell nationwide. The vast majority of the reps you hire will sell within a market local to where they live. When you take on a new rep or rep group, it is essential to define what territories they will be covering for you. This is not a complicated issue since most reps already have an established territory.

But what happens if you find a superstar rep who covers the same territory as someone you already have in place? Like any business arrangement, you discuss it. Some reps may be willing to negotiate partial territories, but some will not. For instance, you already have an independent rep in Southern California, and you are talking with a rep group that covers the entire state. The group principle may not be willing to do partial coverage of the state for your line. At that point, you, as a manufacturer, will have to decide whether to stay with the independent rep or drop them and hire the rep group. We know that may sound a little harsh, but that is how important territory is to a rep. The last thing you want is reps competing for the attention of the same retail buyers in the same area. It is a waste of everyone's time.

We know of many manufacturers who are fiercely loyal to their reps. No matter how big or high profile the vying party is or what lofty promises they make, once a territory is claimed it is off the board. We also know of manufacturers who change reps like they change their socks.

There are few guarantees in this or any business. But please know that if you choose to work with reps, we promise you will be faced with this situation at some point. It is almost impossible to know the best way to handle it. Only you can ultimately decide what is best for your company and the types of relationships you want to build with your sales force.

Our experience has been that the most successful manufacturers are the ones who have long-term relationships with their reps. We know manufacturers and reps who have worked together for over 25 years. Some of them even got started in the industry together. Those relationships have survived all kinds of challenges and celebrations, both personal and professional. These manufacturers and reps want to do well for each other, and they genuinely care about each other in ways that reach far beyond the order form. You may not get to be life-long best friends with all of your reps, but you will benefit greatly by developing strong and meaningful relationships with them.

Accounts (also known as Customers)

Just as territory is considered the lifeblood of sales, your accounts are the heartbeat of your company. You can have the most amazing product in the world, but if you do not have any accounts selling it, well, who cares? An account is a wholesale customer, most often a retail store. Accounts come in all shapes and sizes. They will be brick and mortar stores, online stores or maybe even vendors at craft shows or traveling markets.

For the most part, reps will expect to have all the accounts in their territory turned over to them. Turning over an account means that it is open and available for the rep to pursue and sell to, regardless of the accounts' order history. For example, you have ten customers in a territory, all of whom have been placing orders directly with you for the past year. You hire a rep (we'll call him Matt) to represent you in that territory. You can expect Matt to contact all ten of those customers and begin to work with them directly. Some of the stores may want to continue to order directly with you instead of going through Matt. Obviously, you cannot force an account to work with a rep, but we recommend you encourage them to do so. Remember, the whole point of hiring reps is so you do not have to wrangle the sales yourself.

On occasion, you may want to reserve a customer as a house account. House accounts are those that you as the manufacturer will handle directly, even though it is located in a rep's territory. House accounts tend to be in place at the time reps are hired.

Your rep, Matt, lands you in a 15-store chain, and the dough starts rolling in. Woohoo! Your pupils turn into dollar signs for a moment, and you craftily consider making this new chain a house account. Don't. Matt cracked the account, and he is entitled to those orders and commissions. The same goes for any time you make a rep change in a territory. Cherry picking all the top customers and making them house accounts to avoid paying a new rep commissions is a bad idea; doing so makes the territory less profitable and ultimately less attractive. You want your reps in those stores, and they are depending on commissions to make a living. If you try to reserve too many accounts in a territory, you may not be able to get a rep at all.

There are, of course, exceptions. Say your very first customer was Betty's Card World. Betty took a chance on you when no one else would even take your phone call, let alone look at your cards. Betty has been your customer for three years. You and Betty have become friends during that time, even though you have only met her once and she lives 1500 miles away from you. In situations like this, it is okay to reserve Betty as a house account, at least for now. Hopefully in time, your sales force will keep you so busy you'll have to turn Betty over to the local rep simply because you do not have the time to work with her yourself.

Another important type of account is the key account. A key account is the close cousin of the house account. Key accounts tend to be national chains or multi-store accounts who buy in high volume. They tend to be very complicated wholesale customers who typically receive additional discounts on product. Because of the special attention and discounting programs many key accounts require, some larger manufacturers have an employee who acts as a dedicated Key Account Manager; sometimes this is also the Sales Manager. Unlike house accounts, reps like Matt are involved with the order taking and new product presentation for key accounts and are paid a commission on those orders. The commission rate for key accounts is typically the same as non-key accounts, although it may be adjusted depending upon how much of a discount the customer receives.

We already know that reps can be an important link to existing accounts. However, they can also be an integral part of getting new ones. There are two types of potential new customers: leads and prospects.

Leads

A lead is a store that contacts you directly and requests information about your line. This contact can come via phone, email or your website. If you run advertisements in industry magazines, they will forward leads to you as well. Leads can also come from trade show participation (we will discuss trade shows in more detail in Chapter 11). Leads are the best kinds of calls to get (next to orders) because it means the store is already familiar with your line and is interested enough to contact you.

Make some decisions about how you will handle leads. Include if/then scenarios and stick to them. Spell out your policy when you sign up a rep. For example, when a lead comes in, will you forward it immediately to the rep for follow-up? Will you send a catalog yourself? Unless the rep has requested otherwise (and some will), we encourage you to give the lead to your rep first before taking any action, including sending a catalog. Let them be the first point of contact. Remember they know that territory and may already be familiar with this store. Let them work it. Be sure to include all the information you have, including the source of the lead and any specific products the store may have expressed an interest in.

You are absolutely within your rights to ask that all leads be contacted within a certain amount of time. Ask the rep to let you know what happens with each and every lead, even if it is a stone cold rejection. It may be hard to hear that part, but let the rep know you expect them to follow up with you, no matter what the outcome of the lead call might be. If the rep hits a dead end with a lead, you want to make sure you remove that lead from your database, or at the very least make a note that the customer was not interested at this time.

As a manufacturer, you also have a responsibility to turn those leads over while they are still hot. Buyers tend to have a very short memory. They are bombarded with catalogs and promotional emails daily, so it is easy for them to forget they requested a catalog, or that they wanted to look at your catalog once it shows up. Set and abide by a 24-hour turn-around on all incoming leads.

Numerous manufacturers have told us that leads seem to disappear into a deep, black hole once they are forwarded to reps. It is true that some reps never follow up on leads. We do not know why and it seems pretty short-sighted to us. Regardless, if your rep is unresponsive about lead follow-up, you may need to have a conversation with them.

We still recommend you give the reps first crack at new leads, and if they do not pursue them, let your reps know that you will. The growth of your company depends on leads being converted into customers. Just be sure you state your policy clearly from the beginning.

Here are some real-life examples of how existing card manufacturers deal with leads:

Company A forwards all leads to its reps. They are expected to make contact within seven business days and report the outcome back to the sales manager. If the rep has not responded after that time, the company contacts the store directly for follow up. This is clearly stated on every lead information sheet that is sent to the reps, so there is no confusion. It is also stated in the Letter of Agreement, which we will discuss in more detail in Chapter 7.

Company B automatically sends a catalog to all information requests. The leads are then forwarded to the reps for follow up. If a lead contacts the company and places an order, they are made a house account until the rep writes an order with them. If a rep contacts the manufacturer after the order is placed and indicates that they have followed up with the lead, that account is usually credited to the rep at that point.

Company C forwards all leads to the sales reps and asks if they want a catalog sent. If the rep does not respond within 48 hours, a catalog is automatically sent. If a new account orders directly with the manufacturer, the rep is still credited with the commission but the order is flagged as "Direct".

Again, there is no right or wrong way to do this. Just pick something that makes sense, is sustainable and seems fair.

Keep in mind that a high percentage of the leads you get will never convert into orders. "Why?" is one of the great industry mysteries. Maybe people need free wallpaper so they request each and every catalog they can. Who knows! Keep your expectations in check and remember that leads are like online personal matches: it's quality, not quantity.

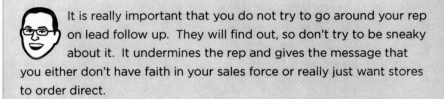 It is really important that you do not try to go around your rep on lead follow up. They will find out, so don't try to be sneaky about it. It undermines the rep and gives the message that you either don't have faith in your sales force or really just want stores to order direct.

Prospects

A prospect is a store that has not requested information about your line but is a potential account. In simpler terms, a prospect is a cold call. There are countless books, tapes and seminars and twice as many opinions about the effectiveness of cold calling. We are not going to weigh in on the issue one way or the other. For the purposes of this discussion, it is sufficient to say that prospects exist.

The easiest way to get a list of prospects is to open up the yellow pages. Another way is to look at the retailer lists of card companies similar to yours. Many manufacturers have retail store locators on their websites.

If you do not have any accounts in a territory you have just hired someone to cover, providing a list from the phone book is not helpful. An established rep will already know (and probably work with) the stores in the territory that will be the best fit for your products.

Orders

This ain't community service. We are in this business to move merchandise and make money. At the end of the day, it is all about the orders.

Orders will come to you in one of two ways: rep written or directly from the customer. A rep written order is pretty self-explanatory. It comes to you directly from the rep, usually via phone, fax or email.

Some of the larger rep groups use an electronic ordering system such as Showroom Solutions or Brandwise. Larger manufacturers with hundreds of items tend to subscribe to this service, and while it does make order taking easier for the rep, you may find it cost prohibitive at this point. This does not put you at a disadvantage or make you less desirable as a manufacturer. There are many card manufacturers who do not use electronic ordering systems and have lots of happy reps writing lots of orders. Regardless of how the orders get submitted, you will be expected to pay commission on all rep written orders.

Direct orders are those orders placed by the customer directly with the manufacturer. They can also be phoned, emailed or faxed in or placed through your online store (if you have one). Please be prepared to treat online orders the same as you would other direct orders in terms of crediting your rep.

It is generally expected that you will pay commission to the rep on direct orders, but how and when these are paid does vary.

Here are some examples from real card manufacturers:

Company A will pay commission to a rep on the first three consecutive direct orders sent in from an existing account. Starting with the fourth direct order, the account reverts to house account status and commissions are no longer paid out to the rep. Should the rep write an order with the account after the fourth direct order, the account goes back to being rep assigned and Company A will again pay out commissions.

Company B requires reps to write at least one order every 12 months with an active account to maintain active rep status, regardless of how many direct orders are placed in the interim.

Company C pays commissions on all orders from rep-established accounts, regardless of whether they are direct or rep written. A rep-established account is any account the rep works, or has worked, within the territory. All direct orders from new accounts, however, are considered house accounts (and thus, no commissions are paid out) until either the manufacturer receives an order written by the rep or an order is received from the account with the rep's name written on it.

Company D pays commission on all orders written in a rep's territory, regardless of whether they are rep written or sent directly to the manufacturer.

As you can see, there are different ways to handle commissions on direct accounts. These are just a few examples. Please be aware that getting too picky about direct orders will get complicated and confusing for everyone. Remember that the goal is to have the rep do the work and get paid for it.

Sometimes, however, a rep's involvement in an order is not clear. It is not unusual for a rep to meet with the buyer, show product, take inventory, and prepare and leave several suggested orders for the buyer. The buyer then generates a Purchase Order after the rep leaves and faxes it in directly to the manufacturer. Does this constitute a direct order?

Maybe the buyer was unable to reach the rep (who was out seeing your other accounts) needed to place an order for second day air shipment and called it in directly to you.

There are lots of scenarios involving the time frame in which orders are placed, and the rep may not appear to be the immediate, direct link. That does not mean the rep is not monitoring or working the account. And if the rep was involved by showing your line and following up with the buyer, shouldn't she get paid?

> I recently spoke with a manufacturer who told me they were going to start paying a reduced commission on direct orders as a way to increase rep involvement and decrease the percentage of direct orders. I wished him luck. I sure would not want to be the one trying to decide which orders counted as direct orders!

No matter how you decide to handle direct orders, please do not think you can play hardball and only pay commission on orders that reps write directly. Despite what you may think, this does not motivate your reps to work harder and write more orders. More than anything, it will motivate your reps to leave your samples in the bottom of the trunk and work harder for manufacturers who understand that wholesale ordering is not always so cut and dry. Remember, when you agree to turn over a territory, you agree to support your reps financially.

Just because you don't tell them, do not think your rep won't find out about new customers who order direct. Chances are that new account, the one that seemingly just showed up out of the blue, found out about your line from a rep who dropped off a catalog. We are out working the territory every day, and we will find out about orders and stores not turned over to us.

Take some time to determine how you will handle direct orders. Then, communicate that at the beginning of the rep relationship and apply the same policy to all your reps. It does not have to be a big deal. If you are not sure which is best for you, ask around to learn how other manufacturers do it. Just remember, it is not cool to change the rules once they are set. Pick a policy and stick to it.

It is always a good day when orders show up, product gets shipped and new accounts get opened, but they are only the first part of the wholesale fulfillment process. You are going to need to pay commission to your reps. But how do you pay them? And when? And just how much of your money do you have to share?

CHAPTER
5

Commissions, Collections, and Sales Goals

Here's the part you have been waiting for. Okay, maybe not THE part, but certainly one of them: commissions.

"How do I pay them?" is second on the list of most frequently asked questions about working with reps. The first is "where do I find them?" and we'll discuss that in the next chapter.

Commissions vary slightly with the types of products you sell, but here are the standard commission rates:

All counter cards	20%
Boxed note cards	15%
Boxed Christmas cards	15%
Racks and fixtures	15%
Gift items	15%

The percentage is higher for stationery/greeting cards because the wholesale cost of cards is usually lower than the cost of gift items. Commissions for boxed cards are usually lower than counter cards because the cards in a box are discounted.

Paying Your Reps

Reps are generally paid commissions on a monthly basis. There are two methods that most manufacturers use for paying their reps: pay-on-pay and pay-on-ship.

Pay-on-Pay. Commission is paid at the end of the month only for orders for which you have received payment. For example, your account, Toby's Toys, places an order with your rep, Bob, on September 2, but does not pay the invoice until October 15. Bob will not receive a commission check until you write all your monthly checks on November 1. As the manufacturer, you are not out any money until the invoice is paid. The rep may have to wait several months to get paid.

Pay-on-Ship. Commissions are paid at the end of the month for any orders shipped during that month, whether you have received payment or not. Toby's Toys places an order with Bob on September 2, and you ship the order on September 4. You would write Bob a commission check on October 1, even if Toby's Toys has yet to pay the invoice. Bob could have placed the same order from Toby's Toys on September 28, and as long as you shipped it before the end of the month, Bob would still expect to be paid his commission when you write your checks on October 1. As the manufacturer, you may have to pull money from other sources to pay the rep's commission up front. Reps will get their money much faster with pay-on-ship.

 Most of the manufacturers I work with cut checks on the fifteenth of the month, regardless of whether they pay-on-pay or pay-on-ship. This gives them some time to get their paperwork caught up and still get commission checks out on time.

Personally, I prefer to pay-on-ship. While it costs me a little more money up front, I don't believe that reps should have to wait to get paid. If a rep is doing his or her job, they deserve to get the green.

No matter which payment structure you choose, from time to time you will have to deal with chargebacks. A chargeback is a deduction in a rep's commission. This may result from unpaid or past due invoices, product returns or merchandise credits. So, how do chargebacks work?

You need to keep track of customer credits and apply them to each commission statement. If you owe a rep $200 in commissions for one month and also have $70 in credits for that rep's customers, the total amount of the commission check would be $130.

Some manufacturers find it easier to track and apply chargebacks with the pay-on-pay system. Others do just fine with pay-on-ship. As a new manufacturer, you probably will not have to deal with chargebacks right away. Just be aware that it could factor into your commission checks at some point.

Commission Statements

When you send out commission checks, you will want to include a commission statement along with it. A commission statement is a list of all the orders on which commission is being paid. Reps love to get money, but most need to know for which invoices they are being paid. Remember, they have accounting systems too.

Your commission statement should include the following:

- Customer name

- Order date

- Customer (and/or rep) Purchase Order number

- Order amount (not including shipping fees)

- Commission amount

- Any chargebacks (if necessary)

That's it. It really can be that simple. You can see a sample commission statement on our website at **www.CenterAisleGroup.com**.

Remember that you are paying commission only on the merchandise sold. You do not have to pay a rep commission on the shipping and handling fees you might add to an order.

No matter what direct order policy you choose, be sure to include a copy of any direct orders with the commission statement, especially for new accounts. This will notify the rep that the account is now active, allow the rep to see what was ordered and use that information to follow up. Most manufacturers will just include a copy of the packing list or invoice with the commission statement and the commission check. For new accounts, be sure to include the telephone number and contact name too.

If you and your reps are equipped to do it, you can email PDFs of your commission statements and direct order copies. This can be a good option especially if you use an electronic bill pay service for your commissions.

It is essential that you pay your reps on time. Now, we are not saying you need to pull an all-nighter to get the right postmark on that check. But we are saying that recognizing the work your reps have done by paying them on time is a key way to keep them. They have bills just like you. Please respect that, even if the commission owed is $15.

There are some months when manufacturers do not owe me any money. Some of them send me a commission statement listing all open invoices; others don't send anything.

If you decide to pay commission on paid invoices, keep in mind your rep is waiting anywhere from 60 to 90 days to get paid for work they have done. They basically trust you to hold their wallets for three months. That is a big deal. Do not abuse or take advantage of it.

We cannot stress enough the importance of not cheating your reps out of commissions. We guarantee that is the single most proven way to retain—or lose—a rep, not to mention your reputation. We are not being overly dramatic here. This happens.

End of the Year Statements

Even if your rep has only earned $100 in commission, it is a good idea to send a year-end commission statement. A year-end commission statement is a summary of the total wholesale amount sold and the total amount paid out in commission to them. Do not feel like you have to duplicate your efforts. Most accounting programs, such as QuickBooks, can easily generate these for you. Some reps really appreciate seeing the numbers; others could not care less. Regardless, it can give you and your rep a chance to review the last year and talk about the condition of the territory. It can also provide the opportunity for both of you to look at what is, and is not, working.

Collections

Sometimes customers pay late. Everyone hates this: you, the rep and the customer. In general, most Net 30 invoices are paid within 45 days. Most Net 60 invoices are paid within 80 days. Do not freak out if someone runs five days late, unless it is a $3,000 order and the rent is due. Then you can panic like the theater is on fire! Okay, just kidding about that last part.

We are big fans of getting a credit card over the phone for past due invoices. The goal is to clear the invoice out as soon as possible. Some stores may ask for a payment plan. Think about how accommodating you can be and, by all means, do not ship additional product to the store before you get paid. Generally, we recommend giving an account up to four months (120 days) before you pull out the big guns.

No one likes collections. Asking for money is right up there with public speaking on the Top Ten List of things most people hate. Unfortunately, this is a necessary evil of running your own business. As a business owner, you should never be afraid to ask for your money.

Here is our suggested Five Point Plan for getting your money:

Call your rep. Ask what's up with the account. There may be behind-the-scenes things happening that are affecting the bill payment. Maybe the owner has been ill or had a baby, or there has been a death in the family. Chances are your rep will know the scoop.

Ask the rep to help collect. This has been our most effective approach. The rep has an established relationship with the account and, as a result, stands a much better chance of getting a check or credit card number. Think about it: You (a virtual stranger) can call, and the account hears, "Pay up or you are going to collections!" The rep (a friend to the account) calls or drops by, and the account hears, "Hey I got a notice that this invoice was late. Can you help me out?" If you were a busy storeowner, which call would you rather get?

Email or fax a copy of the invoice to the rep. The first thing a customer will ask for in cases of past due invoices is a copy of the invoice. Stores, especially small ones, can be chaotic places and things fall through the cracks or get overlooked all the time. Invoices are no exception. Our experience has been that most stores pay up on the first request and never require a second phone call.

Notify the rep if payment is not received. After these steps have been taken, if you have not heard from the account, follow up with your rep after about three weeks.

Last resorts. Depending on the size of your company, you may need to send a seriously delinquent account to a collection agency. Most collection agencies keep anywhere from 20 to 60 percent of what they are able to recoup. If you decide this is not a route you want to take and you have exhausted every other option, be prepared to absorb the loss. We know how awful this is! No one wants to take a hit. Be sure to ask your accountant if you can deduct any unpaid invoices as a loss on your taxes.

 Please do not ship merchandise before a credit card number is processed. Once the merchandise has left your warehouse, it is very difficult to get a new card number if the first one is declined. Always run the credit cards first!

Your reps can be incredibly helpful in collections and we encourage you to enlist their assistance. Our experience has been that they are in the best position to take care of past due invoices. With that said, however, some reps will flat out refuse to help with delinquent invoices. If that is the case, you might be stuck. Of course, you can also nicely remind them that you cannot pay them until the invoice is cleared (if you pay-on-pay) or that the commission amount will be charged back out of their next check (if you pay-on-ship). Let them know that you believe they might have better luck at collecting since they have a more direct relationship with the account.

Reps vary in how they think about collections, so this is an important discussion to have at the beginning of your representation agreement. Be clear about your expectations regarding collections.

A word about quotas and sales goals from Meryl

There is this old school business idea that sales people need goals and quotas to keep them motivated and focused. I say bullpucky. Money, more than anything else, is what keeps your reps focused. Rest assured, they will chase it. Unless you are prepared to pony up a big, fat bonus check at the end of the year, be cool about laying out sales goals. Furthermore, unless you are prepared to fire a rep for not meeting your quota, do not waste your time cooking one up.

Personally, I hate sales goals set by a manufacturer. I understand they can help give manufacturers and reps a point of commonality, and they can serve as a measuring stick of adequate representation. It can be very frustrating when someone on the other side of the country tries to dictate how much I should be able to sell in my territory—which they may not have ever stepped foot in. The only thing worse is a call or an email asking why my numbers are down and what I'm going to do to turn it around.

If a rep is not writing orders, they know it. Every rep out there knows exactly how much they need to sell to make the level of income they want. Many set their own goals based on any number of factors. I have monthly and annual sales goals I set for myself, and I do not share them with anyone; not all reps do this. I am also very competitive in the numbers game, and I have a general idea of what I need to deliver to be number one across the board. Some reps are not competitive at all; they do what they do, however they do it.

I also believe that serving customers with a standard of excellence and working with them in ways that are most beneficial and valuable to them is 1000 times more important than any sales number. I will choose the customer over a dollar figure any day, despite my ambition and greed. By the same token, there are still some reps out there who love getting a number and will work day and night to hit those digits. These days, I am finding those types of reps to be few and far between.

As a manufacturer, you are certainly entitled to have an idea of what you'd like to see a territory deliver. I encourage you to discuss these goals with your reps in terms of the number of accounts as well as dollars. Get their input. Are your numbers realistic? Are theirs? Work with your reps to develop a territory but do not bully or lean hard on them. Listen to what they have to say. Be prepared to hear that things are just not happening for your line right now.

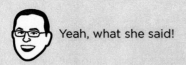 Yeah, what she said!

Money, money, money! All we are talking about is money. What about the art? The style? The creativity? You did not get into this to be a bean counter, right?

Take heart; this is actually an exciting part of having your own business! Every manufacturer we talked to in preparing this book could tell us exactly when they wrote their first commission check, to whom it went and how much it was for. One friend of ours has the first commission check he wrote framed and hanging in his office. It was written for $17.50. To him, it may as well have been for $17 million. He is really proud of both the check and everything it represents. We have no doubt you'll be there, too.

PART
THREE

Finding and
Recruiting Reps

CHAPTER

6 | Finding Reps

"How do I find reps that want to work with me?"

In our collective 20 years in the greeting card industry, this is the number one, most frequently asked question from new manufacturers. It is asked so frequently that it was the very inspiration for writing this book.

You might be hoping—maybe even praying—for a magical spell/method/system to find dedicated and productive sales reps. You know they are out there. Other companies have them, but how do you find them and get them working for you?

The simple and disappointing truth is there is no one all-encompassing answer. We wish there was, because we could make a small fortune telling you about it. But don't despair! Just because there is no one way to find reps does not mean you are without options. The good news is there are lots of ways to find great reps, and some will work better for you than others.

Looking for a sales rep is a lot like looking for a date; you do not want just anyone. When dating, you want someone you find attractive, who has similar interests, and is looking for what you have to offer. The same is true for finding reps. You want someone who has the qualities you are looking for. You want them to have established accounts in territories where you currently do not have representation. You want their product mix of other lines to be complimentary to yours. And most importantly, you want them to be interested in your products.

I had a rep at a trade show stop and ask if Paper Words was looking for reps. The guy then proceeded to talk about himself and the other lines he represented, which were things like team sports jackets and trading cards. He never stopped talking long enough to find out what types of products Paper Words sold. If that had been a date, it would have been over before we'd finished the first glass of wine!

Successful selling is all about relationships, and your sales relationships start with the ones you have with your reps. You are not looking for just anyone to rep you. Your business and the potential rep's business need to be compatible.

Here is another way to think about it:

Imagine that you are remodeling your kitchen. You are going to spare no expense. You dream of granite countertops, new custom wood cabinets, top of the line appliances, and maybe even a chocolate fountain in the middle! Not being the handy type yourself, you decide to hire a contractor to do the job. You do an Internet search and find that there are 500 contractors in your area. Some offer low prices, others promise to finish in record time, and there are some that swear they will do both. How do you narrow it down to just a few choices?

You would not just close your eyes and pick whichever one your finger lands on. You would implement a selection process. You could start by limiting your search to those contractors who only deal with residences. You could narrow it further by looking for those who specialize in kitchens, and you could get even more specific by looking for ones who specialize in granite countertop installation.

Be a little choosy with the reps you select. There could be 50 reps who work in a territory. Some of them specialize in plush animals and wrapping paper. Others peddle greeting cards and other paper items. Some deal with gifts and jewelry and cards and plush, wall decals, ceramic figurines, and anything else they think they can sell. Then, there are those who deal with air conditioners or office supplies. Not every rep is going to be right for your line.

You may have a rep contact you, who swears that she can get you into car washes across her territory. While we'd all love the business, that may not be the best retail placement for your particular line, and that may not be the best fit for your company.

"But wait," you're thinking, "I don't have any reps at all. I'll take anything that would start getting my designs out there!"

Sometimes, something is better than nothing, but do not forget your USP. It is important to choose reps with experience dealing with your product type as well as those who service the types of stores you envision carrying your product. It takes time, effort, and money to get a new rep up and running, so do not spin your wheels on reps who are not even close to being right for you. There are a lot of great reps out there, but it does take some work to find the right ones for your company.

Searching for Reps

You have it all in place: your USP, your sales materials and your infrastructure and systems. Now you are ready to search for sales reps. But where do you start? The answer is easy: everywhere! Here are some places to start your search:

Place a print ad. Place a "Reps Wanted" ad in an industry magazine like *Stationery Trends* or *GREETINGS etc.* Make sure that your ad states the facts (seeking independent reps or groups to represent unique line of angelic, handmade greeting cards in Florida and Georgia), but do not forget to add a little personality to make your ad stand out. Many industry magazines are published bi-monthly or once a quarter, so this may not be the best solution if you are in a hurry.

Read the ads. On occasion, you can find reps who are looking to take on new lines, ones who have placed ads themselves.

Attend trade shows. Trade shows are a great place to look for reps. If you are exhibiting, place a "Reps Wanted" sign in your booth. See if you can get a "Reps Wanted" mention next to your listing in the exhibitor guide. As of this writing, the exhibitor guide for the National Stationery Show will allow you to do this for free. If the show has a "Reps Wanted" message board, make sure to post your information there.

If you are attending, but not exhibiting, at a trade show, check if there is a board for reps looking for new lines and see if any of them are a potential match for you. You can sometimes post an ad there, too, even if you are not exhibiting.

As you walk through a trade show, look for booths that display multiple product lines by seemingly different companies. Chances are good that the booth is being run by reps. Strike up a conversation, but please be mindful of the amount of time you spend talking—both to the reps and about yourself. Exhibitors pay a lot of money to attend the show, and they are there to sell product. Do not impede that process or assume it is okay to just stand aside and wait while they help a customer.

Carry a big, fat stack of business cards with your business name, your name, telephone, fax, web and email address to leave with prospective reps. Ask the rep for his/her or the group principle's contact information and follow up about two weeks after the show.

Do not bring catalogs or samples to leave with reps at a show. We guarantee all your beautiful sales materials will get lost or thrown away in the post-show clean up. This is not personal. After a full day of set up, four days of standing for ten hours a day, and a full day of breakdown, all those reps want is to sit down and have a drink! Your catalogs and samples are going to be forgotten. A more personalized, post-show approach is a more effective route to take. Send a handwritten card, a tailored email, or even make a direct phone call to get the ball rolling on these new relationships.

Search online. The internet is a great place to look for reps. Posting a "Reps Wanted" listing on sites like **www.GreatRep.com** might be more cost-effective than print. Your ads will appear almost instantly and often reps can click through your ad to see your website. Do a search on "sales reps wanted" to find more sites that accept "Reps Wanted" ads. Many reps have their own websites, too.

The Greeting Card Association (GCA) is the U.S. trade association of the greeting card industry. It publishes a directory of card reps and distributors that includes contact information and territories covered. While very helpful, the it is only updated every two years, so some of the listings could be out of date. The directory is available through GCA's website for a fee.

No matter how you get them, we strongly recommend researching any rep names you get prior to contacting them, and we'll discuss that in more detail later on in this chapter.

Use social media. LinkedIn, Twitter and Facebook can be great sources to advertise on and find reps. Posting profiles is free and can really help get the word out that you are looking to expand your sales force. Remember that if people do not know that you are looking for reps, they cannot help you find them. Your next great rep may be a friend of a friend, or someone who is already a fan or friend on Facebook. These platforms are changing the way people connect and even conduct business. Please do not ignore them or think they are a waste of time. For a more detailed discussion about taming this beast, see Chapter 12.

Use your own website. Add a page on your site that acts as your own "Reps Wanted" ad. Be sure to keep it updated with the territories that are available.

Let someone else search. There are several companies, such as Manufacturers Representative Profile (www.mrpusa.com), that will provide you with lists and contact info for reps who match your criteria (e.g. your types of products, types of stores you want to sell to, available territories). You still have to do all the follow up, but at least you can find out more about a rep before you call. While using someone else to find your reps sounds appealing, it can also be quite expensive. As we have said before, please research any rep leads that come your way. A quick Google search might save you a lot of time calling people who are inappropriate for your line.

Ask around. Call other manufacturers and ask if they have any recommendations. They may be willing to share information about reps they work with. Our experience has been that as long as you are not selling a directly competing (or knock-off) product, most manufacturers are pretty helpful. Many even have rep lists on their websites.

Buyers and storeowners may be your best resource in finding reps. They can be a tremendous referral service. Call the buyers and ask if there are any reps they enjoy working with and would recommend. As the people who will actually be working with your rep, getting thumbs up from them already has you in the door and on your way to gaining a new customer.

If you already have reps working for you, ask them for recommendations, too. We know of several small manufacturers who have dramatically expanded their rep rosters this way.

This is hardly an all-inclusive list for finding sales reps but it will get you started. There are countless ways to increase your visibility and get noticed by reps. Be creative. Remember, you do not need 100% coverage to get started. When you get someone who is interested, sign that rep up. The rest of the territories will fill in over time.

Tips on Advertising

We have already established that you are a creative genius. Hey, you've got the best cards on the planet, right? But the art of advertising can be daunting to even the most savvy among us. Whether you are promoting your product or advertising for reps, there are several keys aspects that you should address.

First and most importantly, have a clear message about what you sell and what you do. You are selling your line to a rep, much like a rep sells a product to a buyer. You need something compelling that makes a rep want to find out more about your company and your products.

Advertisements need to get people's attention right off the bat. So while you need to cover the basics, have a little fun with your ad. Show some personality. We are not suggesting that you tell lies about your company to make your ad more exciting. Please don't! Instead, put your creativity to work. Make what you have into something smart that will capture a rep's attention.

Below are two examples of ads. Which one would you respond to?

Ad #1

Greeting Card Company Seeks U.S. Reps
New greeting card company based in Boston seeks reps for U.S. territories. Cards are beautiful and elegant, and are sure to sell well. Contact us for details.

While the ad gets the point across, it is not terribly exciting. There is not anything especially intriguing or compelling. It is sufficient, but hardly interesting and would be easy to skim over.

Ad #2

Fresh, Exciting New Card Company Seeking Representation
Boston-based Fabulous Greetings is seeking reps in territories across the U.S. Award-winning artist and writer, Sabrina Jones, heads our design team. These cards are great for all ages and will prove to be a top-seller for any rep. Visit www.FabulousGreetings.com and let our Fabulous cards win you over.

Now we're talkin'. The second ad gives the reader a bit more information about the company. It promotes the sellability of the cards and notes that the designer is an award-winning artist—both lend credibility to this new company. Plus, the second ad is just more interesting to read.

We know that longer ads cost more money, especially if you are paying per word. At the risk of sounding flip, you gotta pay to play. As we discussed earlier, there are some areas in which you can save money. However, specific, targeted, and well-executed promotion of your businesses, as well as the recruitment of sales reps, are not areas you want to skimp on.

Some people spend their entire lives studying the science of advertising. Your ads do not need to be Super Bowl quality, but they need to be complete. Here are some additional things to consider when constructing a rep recruitment ad:

Available territories. Be clear about what territories are available. If you are looking for reps in a specific territory, say so. If you are looking for reps across the U.S. but already have reps in Massachusetts and Florida, mention that as well.

Type of reps. Are you willing to take on reps who are new to the industry? Do you only want to work with those who have established accounts and territories? What about rep groups? Do they need to have a showroom at one of the major gift markets? As a new manufacturer, you may be happy with any representation, but these elements are things to keep in mind.

An industry veteran told us that the best reps are not looking at the ads in the backs of magazines or online. While that may be true in some instances, there are lots of manufacturers, Paper Words among them, who have found reps through advertising. What works for one manufacturer may not work for another. While you want to work with professional sales people who are going to generate income for your company, you do not necessarily need to go after the biggest and best-known rep groups. In all honesty, they may not be interested in you as a new manufacturer. You may need a few years to become more established before the bigger groups will take notice. While it would be nice to end up with some of those big players working for you, the goal is to get your line out there and make money now.

But will they like you?

You want to work with reps who understand the market, your product and, most importantly, how your product fits into the market. Reps have requirements of manufacturers too, so let's examine what a rep may be looking for in you.

Keeping a lines list fresh is important to most reps, and this is done by constantly adding, and sometimes dropping, lines. A lines list, also called a package, is the roster of manufacturers represented by an individual rep or a rep group. Some reps construct packages that work together, while others go for a particular type of product (such as handmade cards). Others will pick up whatever they like and think they can sell with little consideration to how (or if) the products will work together. Most importantly, reps want to make sure that you are offering good products at a price that will sell. They also want to make sure that you have enough product to sell. If you have fewer than 40 cards in your line, many reps will pass until your line is more substantial.

> When considering a new card or gift line, I first have to like it. Then I apply my "Ten People" rule. I need to be able to identify ten existing customers who would buy it. If I cannot think of ten, I pass on the line. I have turned down some terrific lines as a result of this rule. It wasn't that the lines were not good; it was that the lines were not a good fit for my customer base. Note the difference.

Getting the Date

Once you have found a few reps, get on the phone for a little getting-to-know-you session. What should you say? How do you start?

You can make this much easier by doing some research on the rep before picking up the phone. As we mentioned, many reps and rep groups have websites that contain plenty of information about them and the manufacturers they represent. By doing a little investigation, you can have all kinds of questions ready that will show you have done your homework and that you are confident the rep you are calling is right for you. Just make sure you preface any familiar questions or comments with, "I went to your website and saw [whatever you saw]." You do not want to come across as some creepy stalker. You might also want to mention how you found them. Let them know if they were recommended by a buyer or one of your other reps. Everyone appreciate knowing who their fans are. If the rep contacted you initially because of one of your catchy advertisements, he or she should have already provided you some basic information that you can use to get the conversation going.

Having your pitch ready will make the conversation go much smoother—trust us. You may only get one chance to talk to this rep, so the first impression you make is really important.

Remember to stay focused on the positive aspects of your company. Stress the benefits and features of you product. Talk about why your line is better than the competition and who, exactly, you think your competition is. Discuss the size of your potential market. Explain what kind of support you will be offering the rep, such as a training CD or a customer/lead list. Let the rep know that you have (or will have) a marketing plan in place. Remember that you are trying to recruit a potential rep to work with you, so sell yourself and your product.

Keep it professional, be friendly and, most importantly, tell the truth. If you are just starting out, say so. You do not have to divulge every deep, dark corporate secret. Just be honest about where your business is right now and where it is headed.

Types of Questions For Reps

People generally feel most comfortable when they are talking about themselves. So ask your potential rep some questions and get him or her talking.

If the rep does not have a website that has this information, you might ask the following:

- What is your territory?

- What other product lines do you represent?

- Do you have products in my category, and if so, which ones?

- If they do have a website, you should already have the answers to those basic questions. Take advantage of this time to take your questions deeper.

- How long have you been a sales rep?

- How did you get started?

- What do you enjoy most about being a sales rep and why?

Try to get a feel for the rep's personality. See if this is someone that you want representing your line and your company. And trust your gut. If there is something you do not feel good about, ask more questions or thank the rep for taking the time to talk to you and move on.

A final word about contacting reps

Please remember that most reps have pressing schedules and short windows of time to contact customers. We recommend that you make your first contact with the prospective rep via email. You can attach a link to your website and include some basic information about your line. Follow up with a phone call in about two weeks if you have not heard back.

If you cannot find a rep's email address (or the rep do not have one), give him or her a call. If voicemail picks up, leave a message. Speak slowly and clearly with your name, the company name, your phone number and a short sentence saying you'd like to talk to discuss repping your line. Make sure you leave your phone number at the beginning and the end of the message. That way, the rep does not have to listen to the whole message again to get your number. It is not our intention to be patronizing or dumb-down this point. It is astonishing to us how many rambling and indecipherable voicemail messages we receive.

Should you be lucky enough to reach the rep, introduce yourself and ask if it is a good time to talk. If so, go for it. If the response is no, ask to set up a phone appointment to discuss your line. We have never known a rep to not be accommodating to a polite request like this.

Keep in mind that from time to time reps may put a moratorium on new lines. Sometimes they get overextended or they need to reduce their workloads for one reason or another. Before launching into your carefully constructed pitch, start by asking if they are picking up new lines. If the answer is no, respond with "No problem." Do not beg or plead with them to reconsider or say this is the biggest mistake ever. Instead, ask for a referral to another rep in that territory who might be looking for new lines. Do not take this personally—it is not about you. Remember to be patient and polite.

Finding reps is a never-ending process but if you have a system, you can make that process more streamlined and a little more enjoyable. At the very least, you will make a lot of industry connections that may end up being beneficial. The more people who know the name of your company, the better—even if they do not rep your line, at least they know you are out there.

CHAPTER

CHAPTER

7 Signed and Sealed

Finally, you have landed your first rep. All your hard work, research and phone calls have paid off. Congratulations are definitely in order. You are on your way to fame and glory now, baby! Finding a sales agency or rep to carry your line is a big deal, and you should be feeling really good about now. New love is like that.

Like most relationships, however, the good feelings will only get you so far. To give your reps the best chance at success, you need to make sure they have the right tools to get the job done.

Sign-up Packages

Many reps have a basic sign-up package that includes a Letter of Agreement, a contact sheet with their mailing information (phone, fax, cell, email, etc.), a completed W-9 tax form and a copy of their most recent lines list. Rep groups may also include a list of their sub-reps and the territories they cover. However, not all reps provide this information. Be prepared to ask for it at the beginning of your relationship so you can establish your rep information files.

Letter of Agreement

We encourage you to have a written Letter of Agreement with all of your rep groups and independent sales reps. Expectations, territory, and commission payment details are much easier to spell out at the beginning of the relationship, when everyone is still getting along. It is best not to have to rely on the memory of those dewy-eyed promises made during the first few days, should things turn tough. We like to think of it as a pre-nup.

A Letter of Agreement is a written understanding of the business you intend to do together. This is not a contract, so you do not need to call your lawyer. It does, however, act as a binding agreement that most arbitrators will back up, so do not put anything in there that you are not willing to stand behind.

Letters of Agreement are not the industry standard, but we recommend them anyway. Historically, manufacturer-rep arrangements for greeting cards and gifts have existed largely as verbal agreements. A principle or rep may be a little put off by the idea of a "contract." Assure them that there is no trickery involved and your intention is only to keep your arrangement clear from the beginning. It is also possible your newfound rep will have a Letter of Agreement of their own.

There are very elaborate Letters of Agreement all over the Internet. Many contain some pretty intimidating language about non-compete clauses and proprietary information. As a new manufacturer, your agreements do not need to be that complicated but they should contain the following:

- A statement that this is a sales representation agreement between [rep name] and [manufacturer name].

- Representation start date. Consider including a length of time for the agreement. Some reps and manufacturers start out on a one-year basis. If that is the case, include it in the agreement.

- Territory to be covered by the rep.

- Account management details. List any house accounts here. Include details about how leads and direct orders will be handled. You can also mention the time frame in which you expect leads to be followed up on as we discussed in Chapter 4.

- Commissions. Specify the percentage paid, the payment schedule (pay-on-pay or pay-on-ship) and payment date. You may want to specify how chargebacks will be handled in this section as well.

- Samples and Supplies. Indicate what materials you will provide to the rep. Some agreements also specify who is responsible for the return postage on sales materials should the agreement be terminated.

- Termination. We recommend including a clause stating that either party may terminate the agreement with 30 days written notice.

- A signature and date from both parties.

- You can see a sample Letter of Agreement on our website at **www.CenterAisleGroup.com**.

> I pick up new companies on a one-year trial basis and write that into the Letter of Agreement. If the line is not a good fit for either my customer base or me, or the manufacturer decides to pursue other distribution venues, it is an easy out; just do not extend the agreement. Of course, the decision to terminate an agreement should not come as a surprise to either party. If there is a problem, you owe it to each other to discuss it and troubleshoot well in advance.

Changing your Letter of Agreement

Sometimes things change and you need to alter your agreement with a rep. Perhaps you have added boxed cards to your line, or you have decided to offer rack programs. The commission section needs be updated to reflect 15% commission on boxed cards and displays and 20% on counter cards.

Give the rep a call to explain what changes you need to make and get the rep's verbal okay. Then, simply update the relevant section and have both parties sign and date it.

Please note: Changes to agreements should be done judiciously. Territory reassignments and commission reductions should only be done in extreme situations, like the death of a rep or looming bankruptcy for your company. They should not be done because you think you have a better offer elsewhere.

Taxes and Expenses

Sales agencies and sales reps are independent contractors. Unless you make other arrangements, you (the manufacturer) are not responsible for travel expenses, insurance, general business expenses or taxes. If a rep is self-employed and earns more than $500 in commissions in a calendar year, you may need to send them a 1099. If the rep group is a C-Corporation, you do not need to send an income statement. Check with your accountant about specifics for your state or territory. If you do not have an accountant, we gently suggest you get one. Now.

Supplies

Customers like free samples. A good rep will have plenty of them, along with catalogs, to give away.

Supplies. At the very least, as a manufacturer you are expected to provide a complete sample deck to every rep they hire. A sample deck is a complete set of every card in your line. Many buyers like to flip a deck when they order cards, especially from a line that is new to them. "Flipping a deck" is, literally, looking at every card in the deck, usually one at a time. It helps buyers get a better understanding of your line and it is a good way to get a sense of the visual impact the cards will have on their store shelves. We recommend that you send two or three samples of each of your top ten selling designs to the rep to send out with catalogs.

Catalogs. We mentioned catalogs in Chapter 1, and this is where their importance comes into play. Be prepared to provide ample catalogs for your rep to distribute and mail out. Even if you initially handle lead information requests, a rep may ask for 15 to 20 copies to get started. Rep groups may request more.

Your printed catalog does not have to be super deluxe. We know of many manufacturers who have catalogs printed on standard copy paper. As long as the product images are in color and are clear, you do not have to use glossy photo quality paper. The pages can even just be stapled together. At some point, you may want to upgrade to a slick, fancy, more expensive catalog, but you certainly do not have to start out with one.

Please do not ask your reps to print their own copies of your catalog. Providing the materials and supplies necessary, along with making your line easy to sell, are part of supporting your reps

"Whoa! Hold up!" you might be thinking. "Those catalogs are expensive. Why can't I just use a PDF or send buyers to my website?" Here's why:

As of this writing, websites and PDFs do not substitute for a paper catalog. Period. There are still many stores that do not use email and a few who do not have fax machines or even voicemail. They are not going to see, nor do they care about, your beautiful website, and they will not place an order without a catalog. Part of your job as a manufacturer is to make your products accessible to your customers in ways that make sense to them, not you.

Now, that does not mean you should not have a functional website or even an online ordering option (which we discuss at length in Chapter 12). It only means that at this point you need to have a printed catalog, whether you work with reps or not. Even though a paper catalog is the ultimate selling tool, we also recommend having a PDF version available on your website for those buyers who are more web-savvy.

Even with much of our world is going virtual, the greeting card and gift industries have not completely made the leap. It will happen at some point, but if you want to get your line out there now, your reps will need something to leave behind or send in the mail. Buyers are still, generally, a tactile bunch. They like to touch a catalog, page through it, mark it up and keep it on file. Having a catalog in hand can create a great on-the-spot selling opportunity when a rep is in front of a customer, too.

Let's imagine...Your rep is standing in front of a buyer whose wallet is wide open. Your line is a perfect fit. Do you really want to kill the momentum (and possibly lose the sale) by forcing the rep to say, "Oh, sorry, that company does not have a printed catalog, but you can look at it online when you get home tonight and you are tired, assuming you even remember. And, gee, I hope you do not have any questions about anything while you are looking, 'cause I won't be sitting next to you to answer them."

You want your rep to whip out that catalog and those samples and score the sale on the spot—along with a credit card number. Do not miss out on the opportunity that comes with that established connection because you are trying to save a couple of dollars on catalogs.

Also, reps cannot put their contact information on your PDF catalog. They want the customer to contact them to place an order so they can earn the commission. Isn't that why you hired them? Reps do not want their accounts calling you; they want accounts calling them.

I worked with one manufacturer who had a great line and a fantastic catalog. She sent me three copies. I was instructed not to pass them out because they were expensive to print. I kept one copy at my desk, one in my car and gave one to my assistant. Four months later, I got a scathing email from the manufacturer asking why my sales were down and why I had not opened any new accounts. In sharp contrast, a second manufacturer of the same size sent me more catalogs than I requested, along with a huge box of samples to give away and send out. By having such easy access to an abundance of materials, I was able to open several new accounts. The reorders for this second manufacturer were steady and strong, and the overall results were profitable for everyone. Coincidence? What do you think?

Keeping your catalog current is also important. Catalog updates do not require a full reprint. A simple insert sheet is perfectly adequate. Most card and gift companies do full catalog reprints once a year. At that point, you can integrate new designs and remove any discontinued styles. You do not even have to change the cover design of your catalog when you reprint. Just be sure to include the year on the front so reps and buyers can easily tell if they have the most recent version.

Since I do not always reprint my catalogs at the beginning of each year, I often do not put the date on the cover. That way, if my reps end up using the catalog in two different calendar years, they do not seem outdated. I will usually change the cover design with each printing, though, so reps know when a catalog is new. You can also use a sticker with a date on it to let reps know that the catalog is still current.

Customer Lists and Order Histories

In order to effectively win the territory management and expansion game, your rep is going to need to know who is playing. Be prepared to provide a list of all your active customers and leads for the negotiated territory. We touched on the importance of having a customer database in Chapter 2, and here is where it will come in handy. This list should include the following information:

- Store name

- Contact name

- Address

- Phone number

- Fax number

- Email

- Date of last order

- Other important notes (e.g. they only order cards with cupcakes on them, or they only buy boxed holiday cards)

This list is generally most helpful as a simple Excel spreadsheet so it can be imported into whatever database the rep uses. Some old school reps may ask for a paper copy to be faxed to them. Every rep works differently, so be prepared to accommodate.

If you are a brand new manufacturer or you have hired a rep in a virgin territory for your company, never fear! Just tell the rep it is wide open and to run wild. Do not feel embarrassed or intimidated about not having any accounts or leads in a territory. Everyone has to start somewhere and territory growth is why you hired reps in the first place.

A word about integrity and intention

It is not unheard of for reps to be hired, used to increase a customer list, and fired after a year. Manufacturers then pursue sales directly with all the accounts the reps have opened. Do not do this. This is not a "sales strategy." It is a crappy thing to do. If you think reps do not talk to each other and to customers, think again. And if you think no one will know what you are doing, think again. This shortsighted behavior will backfire on you. The most successful greeting card manufacturers and sales reps know that it is not about the first order, it is about the reorders. Long-term customer relationships help build growth for your business. Quick one-time sales do not. But hey—it is your choice.

It is much more dramatic to point out the missteps of reps and manufacturers. Rest assured, however, there are thousands of manufacturers, reps, and retail customers working in beautiful harmony every day, as they have for many years. The industry would crumble without this synergy. This chapter would not be very instructional if we only talked about how great products, great catalogs, well-paired reps, retailers, and manufacturers worked together to keep everyone in business. That process is pretty straight-forward and we discuss it throughout the entire book. Sometimes, there are problems, and we talk about them abundantly only with the intention of using those experiences to help others avoid similar mistakes and situations.

Here's real secret to working with reps: Just be nice. Do your best to build relationships with them. Support them with killer product and current, complete sales materials. Encourage them when times get tough and cheer with them in success. Involve them where you can. Respect the work of selling and give them the freedom to work in their own ways. Your reps will respond in kind.

Help me help you: Tips, techniques and tidbits

Contrary to what they might lead you to believe, reps do not know everything. They are (at least the good ones) incredibly skilled at conveying a sense of authority, knowledge, and assurance that they know what they are doing and are going to take care of you. For the most part, this is true. However, every line has its own unique elements, and often the quirks and story behind the cards make for an added selling point for both the rep and for the retailer.

One of the best examples of this is MikWright Greeting Cards (whose USP is "greetings that provoke," by the way). Sure, the cards are funny and the old pictures on the front are cool and they sell well. But what happens when the rep also knows that MikWright was the first vintage photo humor company, and that all the pictures used come from the family photo albums of the owners and friends of the company? What a hoot to find out that the unfortunate looking girl on card number BD038 grew up to be their smokin' hot licensing agent! What about the fact that the owners met when they worked as airline customer service agents? Or that the card line was born over a bottle of champagne the day they bought a pica typewriter and made fun of co-owner Tim Mikkelsen's mother's photo album? Suddenly, it is more than just a card line. It is something personal, and the product takes on an added dimension.

Your line might not have a story as colorful as MikWright, but you have something that makes you stand apart. Figure out what makes your line unique and put it together on a checklist for your reps. Your first draft may be pretty emotional, and that is fine. Later you can go back and tweak that list through a selling, less emotional, lens.

Keep your talking points to just that—points. Make them an expansion of your USP. A paragraph about how you find inspiration from your grandmother's ghost who visits you on the third Saturday of every month and that you are all into mediumship as a result is probably more information than any rep (or customer) is going to care about. The fact that the artist is a medium and psychic and the artwork is the result of spiritual inspiration is much easier to sell to a receptive retailer. See the difference?

What happens next

Okay, you have a signed Letter of Agreement—check. The boxes of samples and catalogs have been sent—check. Your reps have the customer/leads list—check. You have shared all your inside tips, techniques and tidbits to help your reps show your line in all its earth-shattering glory—check. You wake up the next morning, run to the fax machine, just knowing it is going to be overflowing with orders and...nada. Zilch. Crickets.

Say what?!

What is the problem? Your line rocks! Where are all the orders? Is the machine not working? Is it out of paper? Did the deck get lost in the mail? Is it even being shown? Where is that rep?! What the hell is he doing anyway?

Before you pick up the phone yourself or call your cousin Vinnie to start busting heads, take a step back and do a reality check.

We understand that you are looking at a warehouse full of product that you have paid for and that you need to recoup on financially. We understand the mild panic that sets in when the phone does not ring for a couple of days. Or a week. Or two weeks. Believe us. We have both been there—a couple of times. We get it.

It generally takes about a year for a new rep to give a line any kind of a decent shot. Have a little faith. Back off and let your reps work.

Although I understand that it takes time for a rep to develop a territory, I also know that when reps take on new lines, they have already thought of several places that will buy your line. In my experience, if a rep does not send in any orders in the first few months, that rep is probably never going to.

Once you have a rep in place, deny the urge to call your accounts directly and ask if they have seen the new designs or if they are ready for a reorder. Resist the temptation to lean hard on your reps about writing orders or blame them for the lack of orders.

To win in this game, you have got to let go and let your reps do what you hired them to do: manage the territory, grow your account list and sell, sell, sell.

PART
FOUR

To Have and To Hold

CHAPTER

8

Your Life with Sales Reps

After your new rep is in place, what comes next? In many ways, what follows is an exercise in patience as you wait for the orders to come in. Even while the rep is out stirring up a buzz and you are packing and shipping orders, remember that in-house support and open lines of communication are important parts of the manufacturer-rep relationship. Everyone involved wants the territory to grow and be more profitable. Only by working together can this happen efficiently and effectively.

Keep Information Flowing

A manufacturer holds all the critical information about stock status, shipments, past dues and new products. Be forthcoming and proactive with this information so your reps can share it with the customers.

Here are some ways to do this:

- Email or fax reps directly with a list of out-of-stock or discontinued styles, and be sure to keep that list up to date.

- Notify reps if orders are held for any reason, including—and especially— declined credit cards.

- Notify reps when invoices for their accounts run 30 days or more past due.

- Notify reps if a customer calls directly to cancel an order or to significantly change a ship date.

- Let your reps know if your product wins any awards or is featured in a magazine, a blog, on a website or on television, even if the coverage is only local.

The information and contact you have with your reps does not always have to be about selling your line. Think bigger. What else can you do to reach out to them? Reps spend a great deal of time on the road and by themselves. Anything you can do to make them feel a part of something outside of their car is always greatly appreciated.

Here are a few ideas:

Water cooler chat. Occasionally forward interesting industry news to your reps or even interesting news about your personal life. Did your kid get featured in your local paper? Did you just read a really interesting article about a looming postage increase? Share it.

Send a card. You are in the greeting card business, after all, so you probably have a couple of extra cards lying around. Send a card that says "Thanks for all you do. I really appreciate it". Acknowledge birthdays and remember your reps at the holidays.

 I am amazed at the number of greeting card manufacturers who never send Christmas cards to their reps. This is one of my greatest pet peeves. What are they thinking? We are in the greeting card business!

Offer treats. Reps spend a lot of time and energy taking care of their customers. We have never met a rep (or anyone, for that matter) who did not like to be taken care of, too. Send your reps a $5 Starbucks card, or a gas gift card from time to time. We know of one manufacturer who sent one of their reps a gift certificate for a manicure after she spent a weekend helping a six-store chain count cards for inventory. You think that didn't foster some love and loyalty?

Send some news. Consider including a rep newsletter with your commission checks. Again, this does not have to be fancy or complicated. You can use it as a platform to talk about new designs or products, update out of stock or discontinued lists, and introduce new reps.

Give props. Reps love recognition, so include a ranking of your top-selling sales reps from the previous month. You will already have that information available to you as you process commissions. Then, include a prize for the top rep with the check and the newsletter. It does not have to be a big prize. We know one manufacturer who would send a candy bar to her top three reps each month. She spent less than $3 on prizes and generated a lot of sales through the competition she started among her reps.

If you want to get really fancy, send out sales awards to your top reps at the end of the year, too. These can be easily generated with a word processing program. You can get frames at any office supply store. We will talk in more detail about sales contests and awards a little later in this chapter.

> Before it ceased operations, I repped a card line that sent a rep-ranking list with each commission check. Years later I was introduced to a rep who upon meeting me said, "Oh, I know you. You're the girl who took the number one spot from me and proceeded to give me a run for it every month for a year!" We have been friends ever since.

Little gestures go a long way with reps. Everyone likes to feel appreciated and acknowledged, and these are just a few of the ways you can do that. It also helps to keep you on the radar. Generosity and working in partnership with your reps make them feel good about you, your company and your product, and that will shine through when they are at sales appointments.

Make use of your reps as a resource to help you do what you do but better. Who knows, they might even learn a thing or two from you. Consider running new card ideas past them for feedback, or setting up a time to talk to them about territory management or to share their best sales tips. Touch base with them about any ideas they might have for improving the line or have a candid conversation about what stores are saying. Give them a call to discuss a new project or get their feedback on a new product you are considering manufacturing.

We had a rep tell us that one of the best conversations he ever had with a manufacturer was about a new product they were considering. He was able to share industry resources and on-the-ground retail experience that improved the launch before it was even finished. The project took on a whole new angle as a result of this conversation, which saved the manufacturer money, improved the product and earned the rep sales. Collaboration, baby. That's the new name of the game!

The longer you work with your reps, the better you will get to know them. Keep personal notes about your reps, their lives and their favorite things, just as you do for your customers. You might be surprised to learn how much you actually have in common with your reps outside of your card line. Some good friendships and even other business arrangements might come out of your manufacturer/rep connections. Just look at us!

Incentives, Contests and Rewards

Our flags (especially Meryl's) fly high on the topics of contests, incentives and rewards. We have already discussed small ways you can recognize your reps, but you may want to have some fun and offer up an official, full-blown contest.

Some companies have quarterly contests, and others have year-long contests. We like both, but if you choose to go the annual route, send out updates quarterly so your reps can see how they are doing. You may or may not want to include information about how other reps are doing. We know manufacturers who do both. You might also consider shorter time frames, like month-long or quarterly contests, although these seem to be a little harder to get reps excited about.

Whatever you decide, give your contest a clear start and end date, and give your reps plenty of advance notice.

Make sure you offer prizes that people actually want, like an iPod, or cash prizes in amounts that get attention, such as a $300 Visa Gift Card. If a $25 gas card is really, truly the best you can do, offer it up. No one will complain when they are the winner!

Set up your contests so anyone can win, not just reps with high dollar accounts. Some of our favorite sales contests include: greatest percentage increase over the previous year, greatest dollar increase over the previous year, most new accounts opened, and most unusual new account.

There are some manufacturers out there who think contests are a waste of time and do little to stimulate sales. We disagree. The best reps are hungry and often competitive. Juicy incentives can give you results. One of the functions of a sales force is to act as cheerleaders for your company and one of your functions as a manufacturer is to keep them cheering. You want happy, enthusiastic, loyal reps who want to work hard for you. Even though most reps have an independent streak a mile wide, that does not mean they will not wave the company flag when a big prize is on the line.

Not all of your reps will dig in and participate, and that is okay. Not everyone is a team player. The fact that you made an effort to make it fun and profitable for everyone is what matters. If you are lucky, it will pay off in both measureable and immeasurable ways.

Understand the Sales Process and Selling Cycles

Selling takes time. On average, it takes from two to six weeks for a rep to get an appointment with an account. Retailers are busy people with very full schedules, and the best reps (which, of course, you have hired) know that being aggressive only results in pushing people away.

Give your reps time to do the job, and trust that they are working on a timeline that makes sense for their area. Not all products work everywhere. Tastes vary from place to place. Generally, what is hot on the west coast usually takes about three years to hit the east coast and vice versa. The middle part of the country follows suit shortly thereafter. There are some products that just never catch on in some regions. It does not mean the product is not good. It just means markets and consumer tastes vary.

Every store operates on its own internal cycle, too. In a modest economy, a small card company can expect two to four orders a year from most accounts. That equates to one order every three to six months. Some stores keep major lines stocked year round but deliberately rotate their smaller lines, only reordering cards twice a year to keep their inventory changing. There are exceptions, of course, but this seems to be the average rotation.

There are cycles in the wider retail market, too. South Florida, for instance, has a very different peak-selling season than New York City, due in part to different tourist seasons. Familiarize yourself with regional market cycles by talking to other manufacturers and by asking your reps what they have observed. As we have mentioned before, reps can be a wealth of knowledge and experience.

The overall wholesale greeting card market also has cycles. If you start with a new rep in the middle of October, be prepared to not see any orders before February or even March. That does not have anything to do with your line. During fourth quarter everything becomes about holiday reorders and retail survival. Most retailers stop all appointments before Thanksgiving and do not start seeing reps again until mid- or even late January. Our experience has been that most buyers do not consider bringing in any new lines during fourth quarter, so please do not pester your leads or hunt prospects during this time or expect your reps to do so, either.

Bear in mind that wholesale orders essentially dry up by mid-December, and your reps will start taking time off. We encourage you to do the same so you are refreshed and ready to go in January.

Communication, Trust and Troubleshooting

Trust is hard, especially when you have put your heart and soul (not to mention your wallet) into developing your product line. No one wants to hear that their work is not good: not you and not even your toughest reps. We all have egos on parade in this industry. Everyone wants to succeed, and reps who work on straight commission have lots of incentive to work hard. You have to give them the benefit of the doubt that they are showing your line and trying hard—every time. Even when you do not want to.

Please, do not hound your reps. Desperation never makes the sale. We all want reorders, but selling takes time, especially for a smaller or new line. Some stores will order early and often. Some will love your product and place an order, only to find out their customers do not groove on the line at all. Every store is going to be different.

Over time, you should expect to have regular contact with your rep. Some of those calls might be about stores, leads, product questions or supply requests. If you set it up right, some of those calls might just be a general check-in, a "how's it going out there" type of conversation. You should feel free to ask how the line is being received in the territory. You should also be prepared for an answer you might not like.

It is natural to want to blame the rep when things are not cranking. Sometimes the rep is not right for a line. Sometimes the line is not right for a particular territory at a particular time. Sometimes a line—or the rep—is just is not that good. Regardless of what the answer might be or how hard it may be to hear it, it is essential that you establish open lines of communication with your reps from the beginning of your relationship. Let them know you value their opinions and then be willing to trust what they tell you.

If they say the line is not getting the kind of sell-through they had hoped or they are having trouble placing the line, do not interpret that to mean your reps are not doing the best they can. It is okay to ask questions, provided you are being supportive and collaborative. Accusations, insinuations, passive-aggressive behavior or sales criticism will not do anything to generate sales and will probably result in you getting dumped.

If you have concerns, talk it out with the rep. These discussions should always be done over the phone. Send an email asking to set up a time to do a status check. You want to make sure the rep can focus on what you are saying and that he or she is not dashing between appointments.

 While you are concerned about how the rep is performing, the rep may have concerns about how the line is performing. Remember, there are always two sides to every story.

Take some time to prepare for the call. Do not shoot from the hip, be flip, or snarky. Think about how you would want to be approached if the situation were reversed. Communicate with your reps in a collaborative "I want to support you so how can I help" kind of way, instead of a "Your numbers suck and what're ya going to do about it?!" way. We are all in this together and no one wins if it gets hateful—least of all, you.

Most reps, myself included, do not take sales criticism very well, especially from someone who is not pounding the pavement day in and day out. This isn't to say you should not raise questions or concerns. It just means you should take some time to really think about what you are going to say and how. And do not be surprised if you are met with some resistance or even defensiveness.

Here is an example of a situation that did not go so well:

We know a fantastic small card manufacturer that got great initial orders. After about a year, they were enjoying a steady business and had a number of reps on board. A couple of territories were really producing, but other territories were slow. When the economy hit the skids in late 2008, things really came to a halt in the already slow areas, and those reps, understandably, turned their attention to their more consistently selling and lucrative lines.

The manufacturer sent one of the group principles in a slow territory an email, reporting how well all the other reps were doing and asking for an explanation as to why that group's numbers were down. The manufacturer asked for a list of all the new accounts the group was pursuing. The principle did not see any reason to turn over this information and did not respond.

The most recent release from the manufacturer had been nearly five months earlier and consisted of eight new cards. No new leads had been forwarded to any of the reps, despite having been received by the manufacturer. One of the sub-reps went to the manufacturer's website and saw three new stores in her territory. These stores had not been turned over to her for follow up and servicing, despite the written Letter of Agreement the group had with the manufacturer.

The manufacturer also told the principle she would only send the requested number of new catalogs if the group would guarantee a certain number of new accounts. She said that catalogs were expensive to produce, and it was not worth the money to send them if the reps could not guarantee sales.

Several months went by and the situation continued to devolve into missed phone appointments between the principle and the manufacturer. Contact was almost exclusively through e-mails, which were interpreted as antagonistic on both sides. The group felt a complete lack of support from the manufacturer, and as a result, the manufacturer experienced a complete lack of interest and initiative from the group. By the end of the representation agreement, the principle and the sub-reps were not even reading the manufacturer's emails.

Everyone behaved badly here. The reps did not communicate consistently or effectively about what was happening in the territory. The manufacturer's expectations about territory growth were not realistic and she did not support the reps in the ways promised at the onset of the agreement. Neither party respected, trusted, or had any faith in the other and the relationship crumbled.

Your rep relationships do not have to end like this. Some inevitably will, but we recommend you make tackling these things as they come up a priority in order to avoid this kind of unfortunate situation. Do your best to keep things positive. Respect your reps and they will respect you.

CHAPTER

9 | Breaking Up

Although you worked hard to acquire the reps you have, some of those relationships will come to an end. There may be times when you decide that in order to keep your business growing, you need to move on and find a new rep. It is also possible your rep may decide that he or she is no longer able to provide you with adequate representation, or perhaps it is a mutual decision. Amicable or not, breaking up is not always an easy decision.

> I do not like conflict, and I view terminating a rep as a potential area of conflict. I do not want the rep to get upset and start yelling at me on the phone. I sometimes start to think that if I just wait long enough, a relationship I have with a rep will improve. I always have to remind myself that this is a business decision, and that while I may have a personal relationship with a rep, it ultimately comes down to what is best for my company.

Reasons for Terminating a Representation Agreement

After investing all that time, effort, energy and money into a rep, why would you want to terminate an agreement? Well, the biggest reason would be because the person are not selling. Note we did not say the rep is not selling tons of cards. We said not selling *at all*.

Unfortunately, there are reps out there who will whisper big numbers and sweet promises into your ear, then take your deck, sales sheets, and expensive catalogs and disappear. You'll never get an email or a phone call, let alone any orders. That would be a pretty good reason for terminating an agreement.

We previously talked about giving your rep time to show your line around, discover how best to present it, and find customers who are interested. If you have been together for over a year, and you have had discussions with your rep during that time about the line and the approach, and you still have not seen any results, it may be time to find new representation. If a rep is not selling anything after a year, it is safe to assume that your line is not being shown. At this point, the rep would probably like to reclaim the trunk space that your deck is currently occupying.

Ending a rep agreement is not something that should come out of the blue. Chances are if you are thinking about moving on, the rep in question would probably agree.

Breaking up is not always about someone not being happy. It can also be about other opportunities. The creator of a line I repped landed a great licensing deal with one of the major card companies. As a result, she no longer needed to manufacture her own cards or use reps to get them in the marketplace. She told me she almost did not take the deal because it would mean no longer working with her reps—the people she credited with buying her a house. She was that loyal! I was sad to lose the line but thrilled for her. Even though we haven't worked together for several years, we are still friends today.

So what are some other good reasons for terminating a rep agreement? Here are a few:

No lead follow up. Your rep does not follow up on leads that you send him or her, or even confirm receipt of them. As we discussed earlier, leads may or may not produce a sale, but there should be some kind of communication about them.

 If you have a specialized or niche line, a territory might become saturated really quickly and the rep might simply run out of viable retailers for you, no matter how many leads you receive.

No return calls or emails. We are all busy, but you should expect your reps to be responsive and communicative with you. Now, if you are calling the rep every day, then perhaps the problem actually lies with you. That situation aside, unless they are on vacation or have other extenuating circumstances, you should expect responses from your reps within two business days.

No respect. They may have charmed you when you first met, but if they are being unfriendly to you now, then what kind of attitude are they displaying at appointments? Is this really someone you want representing you? In this case you may be better off without a rep than having a rep who is damaging your reputation.

Remember that reps are the face of your company. Since you will probably never meet most of your customers, the way a rep behaves is crucial to the way customers view your line. I had a storeowner once tell me that he refused to continue carrying a best-selling card line because the rep was always so nasty during sales appointments. Wow!

Change of contact info. No, seriously. You can safely assume any rep who changes his or her phone number without telling you no longer wants to rep your line. Yes, this has really happened.

I had a rep, we'll call him Frank, who was representing me part-time in three New England states. He also had a full-time salaried position, but he still wrote a few orders for me. At the time I took him on I was in need of a rep in New England. Even though I was not sure Frank was going to provide the best sales coverage, I felt that some coverage was better than none.

Frank and I had been working together for about six months when I was approached by a new rep group. This group had eight sales reps and covered all six New England states. They were eager to have me in their lines package, and they seemed pretty hungry to make sales. In my mind, more reps equaled more sales. But what about Frank? I didn't want to hurt his feelings or make him angry with me. I can be such a wuss sometimes! Just the thought of contacting Frank made my stomach churn. Then I reminded myself, again, that this was a business decision. Period.

I called Frank and we discussed everything. Being a businessperson himself, as sales reps are, he completely understood the situation. He knew the decision was based on what was best for my company. I was so relieved! We parted amicably, and I know I could call Frank again if the situation changes.

Granted, not every rep may be as understanding, especially if he or she had put a lot of work into showing your line and making appointments. But I did not rush into this decision. I knew that I was not providing Frank with his livelihood because the commissions he was earning were pretty small. I was certainly taking a chance, going from a known entity (Frank) to an unknown entity (the new rep group), but I did what I thought was best.

Try a Little Therapy

When couples are having problems they often seek counseling. As a manufacturer, you need to be your own therapist in relationships with your sales reps. If you are not happy, you certainly need to look at how your actions are affecting your business. However, you also need to open your mouth and say something (therapists call this "open communication"). Be a grown up—and a responsible business owner. Otherwise, you may be making a lot of assumptions as to why the rep is not selling as much as you'd like.

Last year, one of my reps on the West coast disappeared for three months. No orders. No emails. No nothing. I was getting a little frustrated. When I finally called him to find out what was going on, he explained to me that his partner of 40 years had recently passed away, and he had taken some time off to get his life back together. He assured me he already had some new appointments on his calendar, and I received an order from him a few weeks later. I felt like a total ass. Yes, he could have called to let me know what was going on. But if I was in mourning, the last thing I would probably be thinking about was selling greeting cards.

Open communication with your reps is key. Rather than stewing in your office and making all kinds of assumptions about what your reps are (or are not) up to, pick up the phone and make a call. A relationship that you think is on the skids might be mended in a few short minutes. If you are having issues with a rep, you owe it to yourself and to the rep to get in contact and simply talk. Do what you can to improve the relationship before you throw in the towel.

My favorite 'I'm dropping you' notice came to me via email. It said, "I think we should call it quits. Thanks for everything." That pretty much says it all right there.

Like you, reps have a life outside of selling. Here are some things that might be affecting your rep's sales:

Life changes. A family death is a big one. Marriages, divorces, and the birth of children are right up there too. Your reps may have temporarily cut back the number of sales calls they make but intend to be back in the swing of things soon. Cut them some slack.

Performance of your line. Buyers are not reacting to the line in the way the rep had anticipated. You both may need to adjust your expectations and figure out the next step. Does your line need to be tweaked? Is it inappropriately priced? Are its appeal and audience too limited?

No re-orders. Your rep may have done gangbusters when you first signed up, but then the orders dwindled. The rep probably called on all the top stores to get those first orders. However, on subsequent appointments, the stores may have been reluctant to reorder because the cards did not sell quite as fast as everyone hoped. This is not unusual and it is not your rep's fault, but it is important feedback that you need to hear.

Too many lines. Some reps are just overextended and carry too many lines. They pay the most attention to their top sellers, not really pushing their smaller-selling lines.

 Every rep works differently, so it is hard to decide what "too many" is by looking at a rep's line list. I have 22 lines on my lines list, but some of those companies literally make only one item that only sells seasonally.

Lack of manufacturer support. Are you having decent new releases on a regular basis? Has it been three years since you published a new catalog? Are you not forwarding new leads to your rep? Reps can only be as good as the manufacturers who stands behind them, so if you are not supporting your reps as best you can, you cannot expect them to do their best work for you.

Not a great salesperson. Like any profession, just because someone is in it does not mean they are good at it. Some reps may get lucky or carry a few best-selling lines that sell themselves. If they are not skilled they may have trouble selling your line, no matter what you do to try to help them.

They are not that into you. It could be that your rep's client base of stores may not be a good fit for your products. Some reps only go to the same stores they have been calling on for years. Others reps are always looking to grow the account list with new stores. Regardless, if the stores they do visit are not enamored with what you are offering, there may not be many sales.

Take the time to talk to your rep to find out what is really going on. Remember that reps are salespeople; just as they choose their words carefully to make a sale, they may choose their words a little too carefully when you ask them why their numbers are not so hot. Reps work for you, and they may hesitate to tell you buyers do not really like your line. It may be what you need to hear, but your reps are not going to look forward to saying it.

Calling it Quits

You have decided that this just is not the right relationship for either one of you. You have agreed that the relationship is not profitable and that it is time to move on. So how do you terminate the agreement?

Whether the decision is made by you, the rep, or collectively to terminate a representation agreement, a simple statement is really all you need. We have seen and experienced terminations via email, fax and the phone. Since your reps are not under a legal contract, you can part ways almost as easily as you got together. To cover yourself though, you want to be somewhat formal about it.

The Letter of Agreement you both signed in the beginning should state that either one of you has the right to terminate the agreement with 30 days written notice. Even if you have already agreed to it on the phone, you should still send a statement officially ending your representation agreement. You can fax it or send a copy in the mail. No matter what, take the high road and be sure you abide by the 30 day notice. It is possible that the rep may have upcoming appointments in those remaining 30 days and could still write an order or two, though do not be surprised if the rep does not write any.

 I once dropped a manufacturer with a full 30-day notice and they responded by saying, "Do you mind if we make it effective immediately?" Guess it really was time for us to part ways.

Keep in mind that you may still owe the rep commissions. If your commission agreement is for pay-on-pay, or if the rep took orders with a future ship date (as can be the case, especially with holiday orders), you still owe them commissions earned, regardless of whether they are still representing you.

Getting Dumped

Sometimes, you are not the dumper but the dumpee. A rep may decide to break up with you. Hopefully, it will be done with courtesy and respect and will not come at you out of the blue. However, this is not always the case. Below are two stories from our personal archives:

Rob's Story:
I had a rep group I'd been working with for less than a year decide to terminate our agreement. The group principle, we'll call her Mary, was impressed with all the materials, the decks, even the carrying cases that I had sent for the ten reps working in her group. I had spent a great deal of time and money getting them all the materials they needed.

The sales with the group started slow but steadily picked up—nothing record-breaking, but solid orders and good accounts. I kept in regular contact with Mary and each of the reps, making sure they had what they needed, discussing ways to improve sales, and providing them with support. Around the holidays, the orders dropped off, which I completely expected.

And then, out of the blue, I received an email from Mary stating that after careful consideration, her rep group was no longer going to carry my line. The sales were not what they had hoped for, and it was no longer worth their time. Ouch!

There was no phone call prior to this bomb-dropping email. No mention from her that she was unhappy. Just an email saying that it was over. Needless to say, I was more than a little stunned and upset. I was not going to beg her to keep me on, but I was hurt that she had made her decision without any discussions with me.

Even though we are in the industry of sentiment, it still comes down to business. When Mary dumped me, she was taking care of her business and not worrying about my feelings. I really couldn't take being dumped in an email too personally. On the other hand, the courtesy of a phone call would have been nice. But sometimes, people are not nice, and that, too, is business.

I did appreciate the fact that Mary was upfront and told me that her group no longer wanted to carry my line. They could have just stopped showing it to buyers. To her credit, Mary gave me specific reasons about why the relationship did not work for her group, and I did take those into consideration when I took on new reps after that. I was not discouraged either. The line was not a good fit for her group, but that did not mean there was not another group out there just waiting to take its place.

Meryl's Story:
I agreed to rep an artist with no wholesale experience. She had not worked with reps before, but I liked her line, it passed the "Ten Person" rule, and I thought I could make a go of it. We signed our Letter of Agreement in early October. She was great about providing samples and beautiful sales materials.

Like most reps, I take mid-December through early January off. At the beginning of December, I sent out an email to all my manufacturers notifying them of my time away. She fired off a very angry response, demanding to know how I could take such a large chunk of time off when I'd only opened two new accounts for her since we started working together.

Knowing she was new to wholesale, I quickly responded by explaining that wholesale winds up in mid-December and stays dormant until mid January. I explained that most of the potential buyers for her line take the last week of the year off, so there would not be anyone around to meet with, even if I was working. I said that my stores had postponed ordering until January to focus on seasonal gift merchandise, which she was not, and that many had asked to see the line again in the spring. She continued to send me long, accusatory emails talking about how disappointed she was in me and my performance and how she had expected so much more from someone with my industry experience and reputation. The final straw for me was when she wanted to see my call schedule so I could prove to her that I'd been trying. The next day, I dropped her. All this drama before I'd ever received my first commission check!

Getting your stuff back

You may want your samples returned to you at the end of a rep agreement. Be advised that they will probably not be in very good condition. If you still feel you want them, be prepared to give the rep your UPS or FedEx account number when you ask that they be returned to you. We do not suggest asking your soon-to-be former rep to pay the postage on returning samples.

 I have never been asked to return a sample deck at the end of a representation agreement. I know a couple of reps who have, but I think it is pretty uncommon.

Notifying Customers

You will want to determine how best to notify customers about your rep change. Some reps prefer to personally tell the accounts they are working with that they will no longer be carrying your line. Some will want you to do it. We recommend giving the rep the option of how to handle customer notification.

If you have a new rep lined up and ready to assume the territory, you should contact each of your customers by mail, email or with a phone call at the end of the 30 days to let them know who your new rep is and how to contact that person. Some manufacturers will offer a sales promotion as an incentive for existing stores to order with the new rep in the first 60 days. Just be sure to tell your new rep about the promotion first!

If you do not have new representation lined up, it is not necessarily a big deal, and you should definitely contact your existing accounts. Introduce (or re-introduce) yourself to them and say you will be working with them directly for reorders until you find another rep. This could be a great opportunity to ask your customers if they can refer you to any other reps they work with.

A final word about behavior

Do not, under any circumstances, say anything unflattering or disparaging about your now-former rep to your customers or to anyone else in the industry. It does not matter how badly he or she might have behaved. Keep it zipped. If you are asked about the rep change, simply respond with, "We felt it was best for both of us to work separately." Period. End of story. Repeat it over and over if necessary.

Relationships of any kind are never easy to end, and alliances between manufacturers and sales reps are no exception. We do not always behave our best in these types of circumstances. And some people will be complete, reality-TV-maniac jerks about the whole thing. Hopefully, you will not have to deal with too many of those types, and hopefully you will not *be* one of them either.

Again, always take the high road, no matter how tempting it may be to do otherwise. Do not burn any bridges. This is a very small industry, and people move around constantly. You never know when you might find yourself in a room, or even working with, a former rep. Keep your game clean.

PART
FIVE

The Business
of Cards 2.0

10 Growing Your Line

Growing a greeting card company is like growing a flower garden. You start with great care in the initial planting, making sure the seedlings receive enough light. You water them, maybe talk to them, and carefully remove any weeds that crop in. Once all the flowers have bloomed, you cannot just walk away and hope it will stay looking beautiful. No way! You continue to take care of the plants— weeding, pruning and enjoying the results.

Just like a garden, a card line needs care and attention to continue blooming with sales. A good initial response from retailers is not indicative of how a line or a territory will perform in the long run, especially if you let your line get stale. You need to keep expanding your line and developing new product. Below are a some ways to do that:

New Releases

The first question most buyers will ask a rep is "What's new?" (followed by "Got any specials?" which we will get into that in a bit). Putting out new designs on a regular basis is one of the top things you can do to help keep your reps and customers interested in your line. It gives reps a reason to call your accounts.

New releases also give an account a good reason to look at your line again, especially if it was passed over previously.

Preparing a new release takes some planning and some serious creative effort if you are going to do it right. First and foremost, make your release count when it gets into the hands of a buyer. Aim to have no less than twelve new everyday designs. An everyday design, also called an all occasion design, is a card that is not seasonally specific, such as birthday, anniversary, thank you, sympathy and multipurpose blank cards. We know that coming up with a dozen new images is hard work. You may need to tinker with twice that number to develop a solid release. It will be worth it. Buyers want to see something substantial with a new release and arming your rep with only four new cards is simply insufficient.

I once received a new release package that contained three new cards. The designs were great, and I excitedly showed them to one of my accounts. The buyer looked at me and smirked, "That's it? This the best they could come up with? Let's look at this line again when they have more to offer. What else have you got today?" She had already moved on to the next line and there was no way to bring her back. She wrote plenty of orders that day but none with that company.

Most card companies issue between two and four releases per calendar year. As a smaller company, you will be just fine with two a year, but be careful with anything less. You will want to time your releases for May and September. Your May release should be the largest of the year and should be available to your reps before the National Stationery Show. If you can manage it, do a third release in January and the fourth should be in July. This is generally when other card companies will have new products as well.

It does not necessarily put you at an advantage to do your releases at off times; in fact, it might actually work against you. Many reps time their sales calls around new releases. Buyers often set up their budgets based on traditional release schedules. We know you are special and like to do things your own way, but in this particular case, it might behoove you to go with the crowd, especially since these release schedules tend to be timed in proximity to peak retail seasons.

I go on an extensive sales tour every spring and fall. On these trips, I hit the stores in the most remote corners of my territory. If you have a release in mid-March, you've missed the first six weeks of my spring appointments, and your new designs won't get shown (in person) for another six months, when I return to that small town seven hours from my home base.

Here is a handy chart to keep you on schedule for new releases:

January	Everyday designs (optional third release).
May	Everyday designs and winter holidays, including Christmas and Hanukkah. This will be your biggest release of the year.
July	Everyday designs (optional fourth release).
September	Everyday designs and spring holidays, including Valentine's Day, Easter, Mother's Day and Father's Day, and graduation.

A little history lesson on the National Stationery Show

Held each May in New York, the National Stationery Show has served manufacturers and retailers as the official launch for holiday cards and the biggest collections of new releases for over 60 years. Many manufacturers, including many of today's industry heavyweights, have made their official debuts at this show.

When the Stationery Show started in 1947, greeting cards were primarily sold in department stores. According to our good friend and National Stationery Show manager, Patti Stracher, the idea for a trade show that focused on cards, gift wrap, stationery, pens, and calendars was the brain child of Tessie Goldwater, who was one of the most influential and well respected department store buyers at the time. Goldwater believed that the stationery business was growing fast enough that it needed its own buying time frame. She took her idea to Bill Little, son of George Little, Sr., and the rest is history.

May was collectively viewed as the right month to hold a stationery trade show since it would coincide with the traditional wholesale Christmas buying season. The show would be held directly after retailers finished with the busy Mother's Day and (sometimes) Easter shopping but before the Memorial Day holiday.

And that is why we head to New York in May. Kinda interesting, huh?

Notifying reps about new designs

New designs are always exciting, and since you'll be in regular contact with your reps, keeping them updated will not be a big deal. When you have a new release ready, send samples and/or sell sheets to your reps. A sell sheet is a page or pages with high resolution, full color images of your new cards and, if appropriate, their greetings. Set your reps up with several ways to get the information about your new release to customers: a PDF that can be emailed, a link to the new designs on your website, multiple copies of the sell sheet, or new catalogs to send and leave with accounts.

Before you freak out thinking, "I can't do new releases three times a year; catalogs are too expensive!" remember that just because you put out new designs does not mean you need an entirely new catalog. Your sell sheet can act as an insert for your existing catalog. This works great, especially with seasonal cards. You can keep your main catalog full of everyday designs, and then add new inserts as the seasons change.

Give your reps at least a two-week lead with new designs or a new catalog. That gives them a chance to contact their current customers and leads, as well as get familiar with the new images themselves. Take advantage of this time to contact any house accounts or stores you might have in territories without rep coverage. Since these stores are working with you directly, getting the new images to them is your responsibility. Be prepared to send them the same materials you are sending your reps.

We cannot emphasize enough the importance of getting new release information to your reps before you notify your existing stores. Do not let your reps find out, along with the rest of the world, that you have new designs when you announce it via an email blast, your Facebook status, your Twitter feed, or the uploading of images to your website. Yes, this does happen. We are not making it up. Be proactive and support your reps by keeping them in the loop.

Nothing is more frustrating or embarrassing for a rep than to get a call from an excited customer who is full of questions about a new release or a new catalog, when the rep has no idea what the new styles are or that a new catalog is even available! Trumping your rep is going to result in one thing: a rep who feels undermined and irrelevant, and that never translates into sales. Ever.

Holiday and Seasonal Cards

Seasonal or winter holiday designs (Christmas, Happy Holidays and Hanukkah) should be available for customer ordering no later than the end of May. Spring holidays (including Valentine's Day, Easter, Mother's Day and Father's Day) should be available by mid-September. That may seem early to you, but the wholesale industry works at least eight to ten months ahead of the retail consumer. Welcome—you are now in a parallel universe!

Most winter holiday card orders are placed between June and August and shipped between August and October. If you send out your new Christmas styles in September, you are too late for the current year. By that point, most stores have already finished their seasonal buying and exhausted their fourth quarter budgets. Having designs ready does not necessarily mean having product on hand. Many manufacturers will use pre-orders as a way to gauge their print runs and may not order inventory until June or even July. Be sure to check with your printer about their lead time requirements. It would be unfortunate for you to have a stack of orders but no product.

So, how will your reps sell the holiday cards if they do not have samples to show? The solution is simple. Just like with your new everyday designs, you can provide them with an easy to read, full color sell sheet of your holiday styles. Most reps can sell off a sheet, especially if they have everyday samples to show the quality of your cards. You might consider doing a small digital run or sending prototypes so that your reps have an actual product for the buyers who like to flip through a deck when placing orders.

Just like new releases, quantity matters when it comes to holiday cards. If you are going to venture into this arena, you are going to need more than three or four designs. Not everything is going to sell. In fact, a buyer may say "no" to two or three cards for every one that they decide to purchase. If your holiday collection is four designs, that does not make for much of an order or give you a notable presence in a store. Buyers want enough styles to give any line good representation and create an attractive, cohesive display.

We recommend you have no less than 12 styles each for Christmas (or the general "Happy Holidays") and Valentine's Day. For the minor holidays—Easter, Mother's Day and Father's Day—you can get by with half a dozen solid designs.

If you have trouble cooking up that many, don't worry. There is no industry mandate that says you have to offer seasonal cards. Whatever you decide, just make sure you do it right and make it strong. Of course, you might also say, "Screw you, Meryl and Rob," put out your three styles and become a millionaire. Anything can happen in this business!

> One way to help boost your Valentine's Day sales and build your everyday collection at the same time is to develop a category of romance and love cards. Leave the cards blank or keep the greetings simple like "I love you." The retailer can feature them as Valentine's Day cards, but after February 14th, any remaining cards can be returned to the general inventory. As a result, you reduce your exchanges and give the cards a chance to sell year round.

Retail customers will expect return and exchange privileges for holiday cards, but that does not mean it is a free-for-all. Many companies put a cap on the amount of holiday returns they will accept.

Here is a sample Christmas return policy from a real card company. If you need a reminder about terms, please see our discussion in Chapter 2.

Orders under $200	No returns	Standard terms
Orders $201.00 – $500.00	15% returns	December dating
Orders $501.00 +	20% returns	December dating

You can see how the allowable return rate increases with the order amount. Also note how the manufacturer has included December dating as an incentive for larger orders as well. By offering these returns, the manufacturer is reducing the risk that the store will be stuck with holiday merchandise if it does not sell. By putting a cap on the return amounts, the manufacturer is also protecting itself against a huge return.

Rack Programs

Call them racks, spinners, fixtures, or programs—we love racks, and most retailers do, too. There is nothing sexier to card geeks like us than a fully stocked, perfectly merchandised card display. The standard rack sizes are 12 pocket countertop spinners, and 24-, 48-, 56- and 72-pocket floor spinners. There are several companies that manufacture card fixtures; we have had terrific results with Wyrefab and Clear Solutions, in particular.

Spinners get you respectable presence in a retail store and are an efficient way to display a lot of merchandise in a small footprint. A footprint is the amount of floor space a display rack takes up. You can opt to have your rack come with a pre-assortment of best sellers or let the buyer select the styles. We suggest you offer both options and let the customers decide which they prefer.

Most greeting card companies offer some sort of rack or fixture program. The way they generally work is if the customer buys enough product to fill the fixture, the rack is free or offset with free cards whose retail value equals (or is close to) the rack price. In other words, when all of the offset product has sold, the store has recouped the expense of the rack. The retail account typically pays the freight charge for the spinner and/or the merchandise.

Below is an example of a rack program from a real card company whose cards wholesale for $15 per dozen and retail for $30 a dozen. Remember the offset is calculated by the retail price.

24-pocket rack	$65	offset with two dozen
48-pocket rack	$85	offset with two and a half dozen
56-pocket rack	$100	offset with three dozen

Rack programs should include a rack topper and header cards, too. A rack topper is a sign that fits onto the top of the rack and identifies the product on the spinner as yours. It is typically your company logo. Headers identify the types of cards in a rack pocket by occasion (birthday, anniversary, blank, etc.). Header cards should also include the company contact information and a place where the rep or retailer can write in the style number. You can also print the style number on the header card when you pack up the order. When a certain style sells out, the buyer can look at the headers and easily see which styles need to be reordered. This is helpful even to stores utilizing POS systems.

Do not be disappointed if retailers do not want a fixture, even though they are buying enough cards to fill one. Stores often have their own fixtures or have a merchandising plan in place. Some just do not have room for any more floor displays. Many stores do not feature cards by manufacturer but by occasion. Regardless, the important thing is that the stores keep selling your line and placing reorders.

Seasonal Specials, Promotions and Other Discounts

From time to time, you may consider running a promotion. Promotions can be anything from free shipping, to extended terms (for qualified customers) on orders over a certain dollar amount, or even free product. There are all kinds of things you can offer to your customers. Be creative.

We know one manufacturer who printed little coupon books for all its customers. Each coupon was for a special deal, such as free UPS Ground freight or a baker's dozen (buy twelve, get one free). They even included a coupon for a free bunny. The manufacturer actually got calls from a few accounts concerned about how the rabbit would be shipped through the mail. To the best of our knowledge, this manufacturer never actually planned to mail anyone a real bunny. The point is that you can have fun with promotions like this while offering your customers real incentives. As always, be sure to alert your reps to any promotions you offer.

Make sure any specials you offer are for a limited time. We suggest running them for 30 to 45 days. Remember, every time you extend a discount, you eat into your profit. There is a difference between offering incentives and giving away the farm.

If you find you only make sales when you offer a discount, it may be a good idea to re-evaluate your pricing.

Growth of your company is dependent on growing your line. The world of retail moves pretty quickly, and new designs are a proven way to stay on the radars of your customers and your reps, as well as in the hands of consumers. It probably comes as no surprise to you that companies with regular new releases tend to get more reorders. Expanding into or offering a wider variety of holiday cards will also gain you access to a particular customer base. The inclusion of value-added elements like rack programs and the occasional promotion will also contribute to firmly establishing your company in the industry.

Even with a sales force, it can be difficult to get attention without literally putting yourself out there. So how do you get onto the industry stage and what can you do to earn a standing ovation? In the next chapter, we will cover some of the ins and outs of trade show participation.

CHAPTER

11 | Trade Shows

A disclaimer: Trade shows require a serious commitment of time and money. You will need a booth design, a booth structure and supplies. There is a fee to exhibit and in some cases a fee to set up your booth. You may have travel and accommodation expenses, too. As you can imagine (and may already know), these things add up fast. There is an entire industry dedicated to helping exhibitors have a successful show experience. We encourage you to investigate those resources and figure out what will work best for you.

For our discussion here, we are going to assume you have done the research and have decided trade show participation is right for your company, that you have a booth put together and you're ready to rock and roll. We are also assuming you are working with at least one sales rep.

Trade shows can be a great place for finding and meeting sales reps. For a more detailed discussion about finding reps at trade shows, please go to Chapter 6. But for now, on with the show.

There's no business like show business!

On the surface, trade shows may appear to be just about writing orders and getting new customers. While this isn't untrue, the real benefits of trade shows often stem from all the things that happen when you are not writing orders.

Having a booth at a show offers the rare opportunity to present your line in its entirety and in a way that you control. You can see what products other manufacturers are creating as well as get a visual sense of trends, colors, design styles and general happenings in the larger industry. Most importantly, trade shows provide the unique occasion to make face-to-face connections with people in the industry: suppliers, artists, other manufacturers, customers, leads and, you guessed it, your sales reps.

If you are attending a trade show, reach out to all of your reps and find out which of them will also be attending so you can arrange to spend some time with them.

Spending time with your reps at a show not only builds the relationship, but also gives you a more personal opportunity to check in with them about the line and how their customers are receiving it. Ask them what is working and what isn't. Ask for their ideas. What would they like to see? What do they think could be done differently or better?

If you exhibit at a trade show, invite your reps to work your booth. Do not wait for them to call you and ask if they can help. Be proactive by reaching out to them. Make a schedule and ask them to work for a couple of hours or even a full day if they are available. This gives you a little bit of relief and provides an opportunity for you to get to know one another better. With reps working in your booth, you may even find your overall sales numbers increase. They are the sales pros, after all. Plus, you get a chance to see your reps in action and see how they sell your line. You might be surprised by what you learn by watching.

If you do not have any reps (or anyone else for that matter) helping in your booth, please do not sit on a stool in the corner with your face buried in a newspaper or locked on a computer screen the entire time. Part of exhibiting is being available to answer questions. Some of those questions will be about your line and some will be about where the nearest bathroom is located. Trade shows are all about being friendly to the people walking past your booth as well as the manufacturers in the surrounding booths. Building industry connections and a customer base is difficult if you're hanging out on Facebook, snarking about how the show sucks and lamenting the fact that you're not writing any orders. Find something to do that makes you look active. Rearrange your display or sort your sample decks—anything to make you look active, engaged, and interested in the show.

Show Specials

As an exhibitor, it is customary to offer some sort of show special. A show special is a promotion offered as an incentive to place an order at the trade show. Typically, a show special is free freight on orders over a certain dollar amount (usually $200-$500, depending how your line is priced) or extended terms to qualifying customers.

You may also consider having a road special run concurrently with trade show dates. A road special is a promotional offer extended to stores that do not attend the show. Road specials are typically the same as the show special and are offered up to three weeks before and three weeks after the actual tradeshow dates. This is a great incentive for existing customers, especially if you have new releases at the same time.

Show orders and commission

When you have reps work in your booth, you will be expected to pay commission on orders written at the show in one of the following ways:

- Pay on all orders written by the rep during the show, regardless of the territory.

- Pay on all orders written from the rep's territory, regardless of who writes the order.

Both ways are customary. If you are not sure which is best, ask your reps which they prefer. Just be sure you use the same system for everyone.

 When I work in booths at trade shows, I prefer to be paid for show orders written in my territory. Those stores are my customers anyway, and I don't feel like I'm poaching off another rep.

With show orders, you do not pay cash on site. These orders get processed like any others. Just be sure to flag them so they can be included on the appropriate commission checks and statements.

If you do not exhibit at a trade show yourself but are represented in a rep group's booth, commission is usually paid to the group that runs the booth, regardless of the territory from which the account hails.

If you exhibit at a trade show and do not have reps work in your booth, you are not generally expected to pay commission on show orders. Some manufacturers pay reps for show orders written by accounts in their territory anyway. This is a generous gesture on the part of the manufacturer and very much appreciated by the reps. Sometimes a buyer will write a show order and request that the local rep be given credit. It is good show etiquette to honor this request.

Treat Your Reps Right

If you have reps working in or hanging around your booth, be prepared to order and pay for lunch or at least do a coffee run. Now, before you freak out thinking you can barely afford to feed yourself at a show, let alone those greedy reps, take a moment and get a grip. Remember that guy at your old job—the one you used to hate? You know, the big boss who always cheaped out on everything and was one of the main reasons you started doing your own thing to begin with? Well, guess what, champ.

You have to take care of the people who take care of you. These little things are what reps remember. It buys loyalty, and really, you can't put a price on that. Your reps are out there taking it on the chin for you every day. The least you can do is show a little thanks and buy them a $5 sandwich. Okay, $15 if you're in New York.

Taking care of your reps at shows does not mean you need to take them to dinner at a five-star restaurant. There are all kinds of creative and inexpensive things you can do to show your appreciation to your reps.

We have heard of rep happy hours and power hour breakfasts in the booth with coffee and bagels. One manufacturer we know hosted a group dinner for all the reps attending the show. Some companies prefer to take reps out for a more private one-on-one meal. Our favorite, by far, is the manufacturer who put together goodie bags with trial-sized foot lotion, a washcloth, and Tylenol. Anyone who has worked or walked a trade show can understand the value of this.

It is the thought behind the gesture that matters most, and your efforts will be appreciated and remembered. Reps do not get to hear the good stuff very often, especially from manufacturers. The size and scope of the action is a distant second to the attempt you make to say "thank you."

I used to freak about spending money on my reps when I first started out. My business was created on such a shoestring budget that I was quite literally counting every penny. One day someone told me that that you have to spend money to make money; I later discovered they were right. By spending the money on meals and drinks with my reps (things that seemed excessive and unnecessary on the surface), I was able to build deeper relationships that translated into better sales. In the end, I actually made money off the people I'd spent it on in the first place. And I saved all the receipts and used them as a tax deduction—double bonus!

Trade Show Sales Meetings

If you exhibit at, or even just attend a trade show, consider hosting a sales meeting for your reps. This a great opportunity to meet your reps in person (perhaps for the first time), and it gives them a way to meet each other. You can use this as a chance to show new products or pass out new samples and catalogs (but plan on mailing the bulk of the catalogs to them). It is also a time to talk about what you're working on next. Use your sales meeting as a place to announce contest winners and award prizes, too. For contest ideas, see our discussion in Chapter 8.

The sales meeting can be held in your booth. Just be sure to check with the show management about any access restrictions they might have during non-show hours. You can also look into an alternate location, such as a conference room at the site of the show. If you live in the area, consider having the meeting in the evening at your home. Some hotel suites have separate bedroom and living room areas that can comfortably accommodate a small group. Since you can easily provide your own food and beverages, getting a hotel suite for a night could be a cost effective option as well.

Post-Show Follow-up

What happens after a trade show is just as important as what happens at the show itself. The leads you gather are as valuable as the orders you write. Once you return home from a show, keep the momentum going by sharing lead and show order information with your reps right away.

Quick turn-around time is especially important for trade show leads. Your reps should have a show leads list within one week of the show closing. It doesn't have to be fancy. You can literally tape business cards to a sheet of paper and fax them to your rep. You will be a total hero if you also include notes with such details as what part of your line the lead was particularly interested in or if they took a catalog.

All show lead follow-up calls should start about two weeks after the end of the show, unless the lead has requested otherwise. Earlier contact will most likely result in requests to call back after the buyer has had a chance to catch up from being at the show. Waiting more than two weeks renders those leads as frosty as a cold call and just about as effective. Even with a prompt, perfectly timed follow-up call, you may find yourself introducing your company all over again. Do not take it personally. Many buyers do not remember all of the companies from which they request information at a trade show. Polish up your pitch and reel them in.

If you do not have show leads for a particular rep's territory, use this as a chance to check in with the reps about how things are going for them. Give them a show report and, if they were at the show too, ask them how it went. If you spent time together at the show and you enjoyed it, tell them.

Be sure to send copies of all show orders to your reps. This is especially important for new accounts. Even if you do not pay commission on the orders, reps need to know what is going on in their territory and who placed show orders. Remember, if you grant exclusives, be sure to ask your rep if any new accounts are in conflict with existing stores before filling any show orders.

We know trade shows are expensive—really expensive—and they are a lot of work. As a new manufacturer, you may not even make your money back with the orders you write. It could even feel like you are just hemorrhaging money. You might look around and not see any of your direct competition exhibiting. Do they know something you don't? Not necessarily. The jury is definitely still out about the continued effectiveness of tradeshows, but for now they still have an important foothold in our industry.

Regardless of the decision you make about participating, think about ways to make the most of your time in front of your reps as well as your customers. Set some goals about what you'd like to accomplish at the show. Do you want to open 20 new accounts? Find five new reps? Sell $5,000 worth of product? Decide what you want and do your best to make it happen!

CHAPTER

12

Selling and Being Online

We all know someone who, just a few years ago, was primarily using a computer to play solitaire. Today, they are a major eBay seller with an e-zine and have over 500 friends on Facebook. They Skype, blog, and order nearly everything they purchase online, from books to raincoats to groceries. Maybe that person is your dad or your neighbor. Maybe that person is you.

The topics of selling and being online could easily fill an entire book on their own, and in fact have. This chapter is far from a comprehensive discussion of retailing and wholesaling greeting cards online or maintaining an online presence. It is, however, a basic guide to help you navigate some of the options available (at least, as of this writing) and suggestions on how to incorporate them into your company and your rep relationships.

Online Stores

Online stores can take two forms for greeting card companies: retail and wholesale. We know manufacturers who have both, though the retail sites tend to see more action. Most of the manufacturers with web stores also work with sales reps. Regardless of whether you offer wholesale, retail, or have an information-only website, we really encourage you to have a store locator option and to keep that list current. A store locator is a geographically sorted list of retail outlets that sell your products. Having a store locator is a great way to promote your accounts, and it is a proven way to direct consumers to those stores to purchase your products.

Unlike Kevin Costner in "Field of Dreams," just because you build it (in your case, a website), they (visitors and customers) may not come. You still need to do a lot of work to get people to know about and visit your website. Since this is a book about working with reps and not a book about e-commerce, we will not go into great detail here about setting up online stores. We encourage you to do your homework before investing a lot of time and money, and there are countless resources available on this topic if you need help. There are, however, a few things we have observed about online retail stores and wholesale ordering that will be important to keep in mind as you explore this avenue—and your future with reps.

Online Retail

We know many manufacturers who offer an online retail option from their websites. By online retail, we mean the ability of a retail customer to purchase products directly from the manufacturer online, as opposed to purchasing them from a brick and mortar store. A brick and mortar store is a retail outlet with a traditional storefront. Some greeting card manufacturers will offer their products on third party retail sites, such as **Cardstore.com** or **Etsy.com**, in addition to or in lieu of their own websites.

With online retail, it is important not to undercut your wholesale customers on retail pricing. If your cards wholesale at $1.50 each, keystone your online retail price. Even if some of your brick and mortar customers pad their profit margins a little by selling your cards for $3.25, keep your online retail price fair. While you cannot always control what a store charges for your line, the last thing any retailer wants to hear a customer say is, "Oh, I saw this cheaper online", especially if that less expensive website is yours.

Online Wholesale

Online wholesale is still in its infant stage, especially for smaller card companies. By online wholesale, we mean the ability of a retail store to place a wholesale order directly with a manufacturer through a website. As of this writing, we are not convinced that the wholesale greeting card market is on board with this option just yet. There are some really exciting web-based platforms becoming available to help facilitate online wholesale ordering, and many of the larger gift companies are already taking advantage of them. How effective these will be for new and small greeting card manufacturers remains to be seen.

You might be wondering how anyone is supposed to keep up with all of these changes and innovations and still run a creative, successful, rep-supported business. Besides, if websites are taking over the world, why should you invest in reps now?

In a nutshell, here's why:

Despite all speculation to the contrary, sales reps still have a relevant and vital place in the wholesale world of greeting cards. That may—and probably will—change at some point. For now, it is still the business model under which the industry operates and the one we recommend for you, too.

There are some buyers who are comfortable and amenable to ordering wholesale online, but many are not. Many customers seem to be using websites only as additional information tools. Many of the reps we talked to said they frequently take orders over the phone from buyers who are looking at images on a website. Even with the information out there and a receptive audience, online wholesale ordering is not a replacement for reps yet.

Remember what we said earlier about the technical fluency of our industry. Some buyers do not use computers or have the knowledge, interest, or time to search online for new manufacturers. Many buyers do not or cannot attend trade shows. They rely on their reps to bring them hot, new lines and make recommendations about what to reorder (or not) from lines they already carry. At the risk of beating a dead horse, this is where sales reps still come into play for you. Even if you have stores that are open to reordering online, don't ignore the added value that on-the-ground sales reps bring to your company and your customers.

I have attended three to four trade shows a year for the past ten years. At nearly every single one of my post-show appointments, my customers will ask me, "So, what did you pick up at the show?" They know I am highly selective in the lines I rep, and they trust my honest opinion about products I have seen.

Sales reps can obtain more frequent orders than websites. Since most reps have their stores on some kind of call cycle, they are in regular, proactive contact with their customers. With employees to manage, customers to engage, bills to pay, and the general day-to-day operations, a store may not even have time to order, never mind scour the Internet looking for new vendors. The majority of retailers (even the tech savvy ones) we know and work with still say working with reps helps them stay on top of their inventory and reordering. That is not to say retailers are not looking at websites; it just means they are still calling their reps to place orders.

You are competing for attention and retail real estate in stores. Many buyers need to be reminded that you are there and have great product, and that is where your rep comes in. We have heard countless stories from manufacturers about retailers who only order once a year at a trade show. Even though the store sells out of the product between shows, there is not a rep working those accounts and keeping those reorders active.

We know several manufacturers who send out regularly scheduled emails to their retail accounts. While an email might help remind a store to check their inventory, relying on email as a form of account management makes a lot of assumptions, including a) the buyer uses email to begin with, b) the buyer sees or reads the email at all, and c) the buyer takes the time to check inventory and put together a reorder. That is a lot of work for the buyer! Having a rep on the ground does all that work for them—and gets you the order. Even with the potential hassles and headaches that come with reps, there are many more advantages to having a living, breathing, caring, person taking your product directly to a buyer.

I have seen a dramatic increase in the frequency and size of reorders from territories in which I now have reps. Even dormant accounts have started ordering again! My email blasts and direct phone calls did not yield those kinds of results. Stationery is still a person-to-person industry.

It is easy to abandon filled online shopping carts. You have probably done it yourself: the phone rings, your kid has a question or you get distracted by something else. Reps get the order and send it in. This means an active, stocked account (and money) for you—and the rep. Remember, a paid rep is a happy rep.

Even the fanciest, sexiest, most sophisticated website can, ultimately, only answer questions and then let the buyer purchase a product. The most enticing product description and slickest graphics are still impersonal, and the number one sales tool your rep has is the personal relationship with the buyer. As we have said before, it is easy to discount the importance of this intangible aspect of selling, especially if you have never worked in sales before. There is no doubt it is the single most important factor in sales success.

Faster, cheaper, smarter, better is the road all commerce is barreling down. The online marketplace is certainly one way to participate. We know many manufacturers who have online stores (both retail and wholesale) and many who do not. How essential this is continues to be debated, being equally embraced and resisted. Like it or not, the Internet will continue transforming the way we do business. If you are not ready for an online store, it is okay, but some sort of online presence is non-negotiable. Social media is another option to consider.

Social media

Simply put, if you are in business and you want your business to grow, participation in social media is the easiest, most cost effective action you can take to promote your line. No matter where you are in your business development, social media is inescapable and your participation is inevitable. Go ahead and take the leap; resistance is futile.

Facebook has over 87 million users. If Facebook was a country, it would be the fourth largest nation in the world. LinkedIn is not too far behind, with over 60 million users. No one knows for sure how big Twitter is, but in December 2008, they reported 4.43 million unique visitors in one month. Technorati reported in February 2008 that it was tracking 112.8 million English-language blogs. That is a lot of people! It is also a lot of potential customers you can access for free.

Even if you think Facebook, Twitter, LinkedIn and all things online are stupid or a waste of time, please note, and note well: these guys are not going anywhere. In fact, they are going to get bigger and become even more powerful venues for businesses in the future.

Just as an example of how far these platforms can reach, we held a contest and collected votes to determine the title of this book. We promoted the contest on our respective Facebook and Twitter accounts and collected the votes with a poll hosted on Meryl's blog, *Road Rage*. In less than one week, we received nearly 200 votes, many from people we did not know. Some of them even went on to become consulting clients.

As a wholesaler, you absolutely should establish yourself in social media. If you do it right, a blog, Facebook page, Twitter feed or LinkedIn profile will boost your visibility in ways you cannot imagine. There are dozens, if not hundreds, of books and thousands of articles and blogs online loaded with suggestions, tips, strategies and guidance about taming this virtual beast. We encourage you to learn and explore as much as you can to maximize these free advertising channels.

Getting started does not have to be a huge undertaking. Facebook and Twitter are incredibly user-friendly. If you are already using them, you know this. If you are not a current user, do not be intimidated. These websites have plenty of easy-to-follow tutorials and help pages. Just click and learn. If you have or know any kids, ask them to show you how these sites work. You can bet they already know how to use them.

Starting a blog is also easy. There are several hosting platforms available including Blogger, WordPress and LiveJournal. Many of these can be integrated with your current website and come with the ability to monitor the number of visitors. These platforms also have a tagging feature that helps make your entries readable by search engines like Google.

Using social media

It is important to have a plan for using social media. Take some time to see how other manufacturers are using their blogs and profiles. Look at both national brands and smaller companies. Check out how retailers, both large and small, are using these platforms, too. What are they doing well? Are their updates compelling? Informative? Fluff? What do you like about the information they post? What would you like to see more of? Less of?

As you start to develop your online presence, take some time to think about what you want social media to do for you. Develop goals and objectives and figure out ways to assess the results of your efforts. The most obvious goal is to promote your company. But there are other kinds of objectives to consider, such as building a community of loyal, dedicated fans or using your profile to attract retailers and sales reps. Some goals can be more concrete, such as obtaining a certain number of followers or friends or increasing your mailing list by a certain percentage.

Whatever you are setting out to achieve, keep in mind that with social media, quality is more important than quantity. For instance, you may quickly amass 1000 followers on Twitter, but if 973 of them are 18-year-old girls or technology manufacturers trying to sell you something, the application is not really working for you. You want to build a list of friends and followers who are interested in and care about your product.

 On Facebook, I have an "accept all" friend request policy. Even if I have never met you, I will friend you on Facebook. I am much more selective on Twitter and only follow greeting card, gift, and occasionally sales-related people.

Once you have identified your goals, you can start to decide what kinds of things are appropriate to post. Will you talk about your development process? Announce new designs? Unveil your new rack program? Are you looking to get feedback on new designs? Will you link to your most recent blog entry? Will you have a contest to write a greeting for a particular card? Announce new retailers carrying your cards? Invite people to send you pictures of themselves with your cards? Do you want to direct people to the store locator on your website?

We recommend only posting content related to your product, your customers, your reps, and general industry information on your business profile. Your industry friends and followers want to read about the cool things happening with your line, not the big night out with your honey, your Mafia Wars updates, or your new puppy. Okay, maybe your puppy. If you want to post about your bad mood, your hangover or what you had for lunch, keep it on your personal feeds.

With your goals and content guidelines in place, you may find it helpful to develop a posting strategy as well. How often are you going to post updates? Every day? Twice a day? Once a week? Every hour? Unless you are a full-time web monitor, set a posting schedule. Social media can be an incredible time suck, and you have a company to run.

Predetermining when you will post updates can definitely help keep this aspect of your business manageable. There are some terrific third party applications available that will allow you to write posts and schedule them in advance. We both like and use HootSuite. Plus, you can always go in and alter your post content and schedules if you need to.

I am a huge fan of HootSuite. It allows me to write a week's worth of updates and schedule them in advance to post at key times. While I'm calling accounts or packing up orders, my Facebook and Twitter accounts are being updated automatically. Plus, I can update Facebook, Twitter, and LinkedIn all at the same time!

Getting Connected

Goals, content and posting do not matter a hill of beans if you do not have a profile set up. Below are a few simple guidelines for the three main platforms being used today.

Create a LinkedIn profile. LinkedIn is a great way to meet and get connected to other people in the industry. Creating a profile is pretty straightforward. After you have a profile, you can connect with others you know by asking them to join your network. Once they join, you can then see to whom they are connected to. As we mentioned earlier, perhaps your new rep is connected to someone whom you already know.

LinkedIn also hosts online groups you can join. As of this writing, there are several groups for greeting cards and sales. You can join these groups, post content, or just receive updates when other group members post news.

Set up a Facebook Fan Page. A Fan Page is different from a personal page. A Fan Page is designed for organizations to broadcast information in an official, public manner. It also allows for a professional/personal distinction. You can post updates on a Fan Page but cannot contact people personally through one.

In order to have a Fan Page, you must set up a personal account. Your Fan Page should be your business name and include pertinent information about your company. There is an information fill-in form that comes with the set up process that makes this really easy. Remember, just because a field is offered does not mean you have to fill it in. If you run your business from your home and you are not comfortable listing your home address, leave that field blank. Do include your business telephone number.

Just because you set up a personal account does not mean you have to use it. Please do not let your personal aversion to being on Facebook get in the way of the professional benefits.

Set up a Twitter account. Much like Facebook, getting started is easy. On Twitter, you can create an account by using your business name. Unlike Facebook, you do not need a personal user account to set up a business account.

Add a button. All of these sites have the option of embedding a "Follow Me" button on your website. They are free and easy to download. Once they are on your website, customers can click the button and be redirected to your respective LinkedIn, Facebook and Twitter accounts. This is a great way to build your Fans List and Followers. This option allows people who already love your products to keep up with what you are working on and share it with their friends.

A word about personal pages and online behavior

We have all heard stories about, or even seen, some of the crazy things people post online. At the risk of sounding like a couple of fuddy-duddies, please think carefully about what you post, both personally and on your company profiles. Your professional image matters and once Google indexes your content, it is out there forever. We are not saying you can't have fun online; you certainly should! Just use some sense about what you post and who can see it.

We have an industry friend who is a former dancer. She has lots of great photos from her years of performing posted on her personal Facebook page. In a number of those photos, she shows a lot of skin. She decided those were not the type of photos she wants her reps or customers having access to. She has lots of non-industry friends online and was starting to feel like her worlds were colliding.

To solve the problem, she created a Fan Page and a LinkedIn profile for her business. She then sent a Facebook message to all her industry-related friends, saying she was closing down her personal page and inviting them to become a fan on her Fan Page. After about a week, she unfriended all of her professional contacts, leaving only non-work and online friends on her Friends List. She used Facebook's privacy options to restrict page access only to people on her friends list. Now, if any of her professional contacts send her a friend request, she replies and explains that her personal page is restricted, then invites them to join her Fan Page. So far, she has found that people are very understanding. Even though it requires an extra step, maintaining a personal/professional boundary has made a big difference for her. She feels more in control of her public image and content and is still able to have fun online with her friends.

We encourage you to follow this example. If you want to post personal photos, make sure you keep your personal Facebook page filtered for your friends only. The rest of us do not want to see you in a thong. Really, we don't.

> I am a big Facebook and Twitter fan, and I post on a daily basis. Even though I have a personal page, I use it for business purposes. For the most part, my status updates are all business and sales related. Many of my customers are also my Facebook friends as well as my personal friends. As a result, I occasionally post things of a more personal nature such as a new restaurant I tried or a place I visited. I am very mindful of my online profile, though, and I do not post anything I wouldn't talk about at an appointment.

If you find a rep on a social networking site, please do not attempt to pick them up via a public feed. Public wall postings begging them to pick up your line or visit your website are not cute or clever. They are awkward, inappropriate, annoying and will more than likely be ignored. If you do not have a rep's email and it is not included in the profile, send a private message. Ask to set up a phone appointment to discuss your line. Please, have some dignity, no matter how desperate you may feel.

In the not so distant future, the Internet will change the face of wholesale and manufacturing in the same sweeping ways it has altered retail. LinkedIn, Facebook and Twitter are already bringing communities together in unprecedented ways. It is just a matter of time before companies figure out how to capitalize on that and, in fact, some of them already have.

With all that said, we know that just because there are lots of people using social media does not mean they are all using it well. If you are not sure of the best way to use these platforms, take some time to see how other people are taking advantage of them. There is no rule that says you have to participate from the moment you join. Settle in and look around. You will quickly get a sense of what works and what wastes your time. Once you start to get an idea of how these virtual worlds operate, it will not take long before you will be finding ways to put social media to work for you and your company.

Conclusion

When he found out we were writing this book, an industry friend of ours said, "Be sure to tell them they'll put out a lot more money than they'll make; there's no rhyme or reason as to when people order; most of this business is pure insanity. Oh, and that this is the best job I've ever had!"

We completely agree—at least about the job part.

Selling cycles, rep motivation, support and attention, customer interest and consumer spending are all unpredictable and elusive. Our experience in this industry has shown us that about the time you get everything figured out, the rules change and you're back to square one again. Add things like Facebook, Twitter, iPhone apps and eCards into the mix, and it can be a little overwhelming. So, if you feel like you're lost and confused, you're not alone. Even the big guys are feeling a little lost these days.

There is a lot to take in and consider when you're getting started, but don't be intimidated. In any venture, especially starting a business, the initial groundwork is the most daunting. You might be overwhelmed with new information, including learning a new vocabulary and getting familiar with the rules of the road. Have no fear. Don't expect to know everything at this point. The reps you meet and the reps you hire will help teach you what you're lacking. Lots of people have had long and successful careers in this business. There is no reason why you can't be one of them.

You will have false starts. You will have big wins. Some days you'll wonder why you got into this thing in the first place. Achieving the success you want may require some flexibility. It might require some reinvention. It could entail some things you (and we) can't even imagine at this point. We've certainly experienced our own moments of doubt. Neither of us ever dreamed we'd be writing a book or providing sales training when we started in this industry. Dr. Seuss was right: How exciting to think of the places you'll go!

There are, of course, no guarantees. You may follow our guide to the letter and still not have the success you want. You may have trouble finding reps or have difficulty getting reps to take your line. It can seem like a catch-22: reps are hesitant to pick up your line if you aren't established, and it can be hard to get established without any reps. Don't worry and don't give up. Always keep working to improve your product. Sometimes having a great line is all about timing.

You may be one of the those manufacturers who attracts a number of reps early on and rides happily off into the sunset. We wish you that kind of luck. More than likely, you'll be out there clamoring for rep attention and doing all you can to keep the reps you have interested in and selling your line to new and existing retail accounts. You'll fret about the numbers. You'll worry about the inventory levels. Some days you might have to pick up the phone to make sure the thing is still turned on. But in the end, you'll wake up every morning, check the fax machine, box up those orders, sketch out new designs, and keep searching for ways to push the envelope one more day.

And the good news is, just because you've reached the end of this book, you still don't have to go it alone. You can get more support at our website at www.CenterAisleGroup.com. Send us an email, sign up for our newsletter, and stay connected to the industry.

With a little care and feeding, you can have a kick-ass rep force worrying about territory and account management and wrangling your sales. Your time and efforts can be put to use doing the thing you do best: creating the most amazing greeting cards on the planet.

We wish you nothing but success!

Glossary

Account: A wholesale customer, most often a retail store.

Blank cards: Greeting cards without words inside the card. May or may not have text on the front of the card.

Brick and mortar store: A retail outlet with a traditional storefront.

C.O.D.: "Cash On Delivery." An order is sent and the shipping company collects payment at the time of delivery to the customer.

Counter cards: The industry term for cards not boxed. Typically merchandised on a card rack or spinner.

Chargeback: A deduction in a rep's commission.

Commission: A percentage of the wholesale price paid to a sales rep as compensation.

Commission statement: A list of all the orders on which commission is being paid. Will also include any chargebacks, if necessary.

Company prefix: The first six to ten digits of a UPC code.

Company rep: A sales rep who works directly for a manufacturer and is usually paid a base salary plus commission.

December dating: An invoice due December 1, regardless of the merchandise ship date. Typically used for holiday cards.

Digital printing: A process where images are transferred from a computer file through a printer with commercial quality results.

Direct order: Wholesale orders placed by the customer directly with the manufacturer. They can be phoned, emailed or faxed in or may come in via an online store.

Everyday design: A card that is not seasonally specific, such as birthday, anniversary, thank you or sympathy. Also called all occasion.

Exchange: The swap out of certain designs for others.

Exclusives: When a retailer agrees to carry a line and, in exchange, a manufacturer agrees to not sell that line to other retailers in a given area. Also called protecting territory.

Footprint: The amount of floor space a display rack takes up.

Flipping a deck: The physical act of looking at every card in the deck, usually one at a time.

Greeted cards: Greeting cards with text inside the card.

Group principle: The head of a rep group, often the owner of the company.

Headers: A card that identifies the pockets on a card rack by occasion or type—birthday, anniversary, blank, etc.

House account: Wholesale customers handled directly by a manufacturer even though the customer is located in an active rep's territory.

Independent rep: Sales reps who generally work alone and are self-employed.

Inventory: A list of products or merchandise on hand.

Key account: Wholesale customers who tend to be high volume and typically receive additional discounts and special credit terms.

Keystone: Doubling the wholesale price to determine the retail price.

Lines list: The roster of manufacturers represented by a sales rep. Also called a package or a lines package.

Lead: Someone who contacts a manufacturer or rep directly and requests information about a product line.

Letter of agreement: A written document specifying the details of a manufacturer-rep relationship.

Net 30: The invoice is due within 30 days of the invoice date.

Net 45: The invoice is due within 45 days of the invoice date.

Net 60: The invoice is due within 60 days of the invoice date.

Online retail: The ability of the consumer to purchase products directly from a manufacturer online.

Online wholesale: The ability of a retail store to place a wholesale order with a manufacturer directly online.

Price point: The retail price of the item.

Price sheet: An information page containing information about how your line is sold.

Pro forma invoice: An invoice that is sent to a customer who, in turn, sends a check to the manufacturer. Merchandise is shipped once the manufacturer receives the check.

Prospect: A wholesale customer who has not requested information about your line but could be a potential account. Also known as a cold call.

Rack topper: A sign that fits onto the top of a rack, typically a company logo.

Rep groups: Managed by a group principle. Tend to cover large geographical territories and can be made up of two to 40 or more reps. Also called a sales agency.

Rep-established account: Any account a rep works (or has worked) within their territory.

Rep-written order: A wholesale order sent to the manufacturer from the rep, usually via phone, fax or email.

Return: Removing product from a store for a refund or credit.

Road special: A promotional offer extended to stores that do not attend a trade show.

Sales agency: See rep group.

Sales rep: A person hired to represent a manufacturer and sell its merchandise in a particular geographical area. Also known as a sales representative or a manufacturers representative.

Sample deck: Sometimes referred to as a deck. A complete set of every card in a line.

Sell sheet: A page, or pages, with high resolution, full color card images and greetings.

Shopworn cards: Cards damaged or dirtied by normal shopper wear and tear.

Show special: A promotional offer available as an incentive to place an order at a trade show.

Showroom: Similar to a trade show booth. Hosted and staffed by sales reps in their home city.

Sub rep: An employee of a rep group.

Store locator: A geographically sorted list of retail outlets that sell a manufacturer's products and that is included on the manufacturer's company website.

Style number: An internal code manufacturers create that identifies a design in their inventory.

Territory: The geographical area in which a rep sells.

Unique Selling Position: Also known as a Unique Selling Proposition or USP. What sets a manufacturer's product apart from the competition and gives people a reason to buy. It defines the manufacturer's mission, purpose and identity.

UPC: A unique bar code that consists of 12 numbers and identifies a manufacturer and product. Used by retailers to track inventory.

Year-end commission statement: An annual summary of the total wholesale amount sold and the total amount paid out in commissions to a rep.

Index

Acknowledgements

We would like to thank the following people for all of their help and support on this project: Jay Blumenfeld, Vanessa Harnik, Cathy Henry, Beth Safran, and Chuck Temple for their invaluable feedback on the early drafts. Tim Mikkelsen and Phyllis Wright-Herman for their encouragement and contributions. Greg Sargent for helping to fill in the information gaps. David Burton for being a terrific practice audience and providing invaluable direction. Patti Stratcher for believing in the importance of this project. Stephen Corsello for graphic design and layout and, especially, Kelli Stein and Sally Ann Murphy for gentle, but firm, editing and ego support.

Rob would like to extend a special thanks to Doll Barnes, Tracey Cook, Erin Rogers Pickering, and Cheryl Phelps for getting him to where he is today.

Our deepest appreciation and gratitude to our partners, both in crime and in matters of the heart, Stephen Corsello and Kyle Todd. Your faith in us, and your exceptional patience, are unmatched. Thank you for indulging, listening endlessly and letting us believe you understand what we're talking about in the first place.

And finally, a very special thank you to all of our customers, manufacturer, sales managers, and rep friends. Your questions, complaints, musings, and general love of this crazy industry were the inspiration for writing this book. We couldn't have done any of this without all of you.

About the Authors

Rob Fortier is the owner and creative director of Paper Words. His card designs have earned him write-ups in industry magazines such as *GREETINGS etc*, *Gifts & Decorative Accessories*, *Art Buyer*, *Giftware News* and *Stationery Trends*, and have been featured on the HGTV cable network.

Meryl Hooker is an award-winning manufacturer's representative, writer and sales rockstar. She is the author of *Road Rage*, a blog about repping, selling and killer customer service.

Both can be reached via **www.CenterAisleGroup.com**

CPSIA information can be obtained at www.ICGtesting.com
Printed in the USA
BVOW031846280513

321830BV00004B/197/P